P9-CDB-836

NEW STITCHES FOR NEEDLECRAFT

Edith John

Dover Publications, Inc.
New York

To
my parents

Acknowledgment

I acknowledge with gratitude Mr G E Brumfitt, ARCA, Principal of the College of Art, Doncaster, for giving me permission to illustrate this book with photographs of students' work, Mr Eric Platt, ARCA, and Mrs Platt who have with their usual kindness and consideration assisted me in many ways, Mr Desmond Byrne, Mr Alec Hainsworth and Mr Peter Sanderson for their excellent photographs, and last but certainly not least I am indebted to students and friends for allowing me to discuss their embroideries in the text.

I offer to all these people my sincere thanks for their help and unswerving loyalty.

Doncaster 1968   E.J.

Copyright © 1968 by Edith John.
All rights reserved under Pan American and International Copyright Conventions.

Published in Canada by General Publishing Company, Ltd., 30 Lesmill Road, Don Mills, Toronto, Ontario.
Published in the United Kingdom by Constable and Company, Ltd., 10 Orange Street, London WC 2.

This Dover edition, first published in 1973, is an unabridged republication of the work first published in 1968 under the title *Ideas for Needlecraft*. This edition is published through special arrangement with B. T. Batsford, Ltd., 4 Fitzhardinge Street, London, the original publishers.

International Standard Book Number: 0-486-22971-8
Library of Congress Catalog Card Number: 73-84801

Manufactured in the United States of America
Dover Publications, Inc.
180 Varick Street
New York, N.Y. 10014

Contents

PLATE I

Burse of patchwork

Doris Warr

PLATE II

Embroidered box

Doris Warr

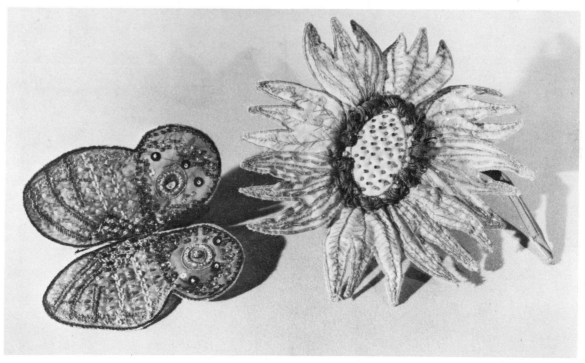

Mobile

Honor Costelloe

PLATE III

The lid and sides of a gold work box showing the overspill from the top   Constant Norris

PLATE IV

Completed box   Constant Norris

PLATE V

'Sunspots' Note raised loop stitch, patchwork and appliqué

PLATE VI

'Peeled Orange' Mobile
Olive Smith

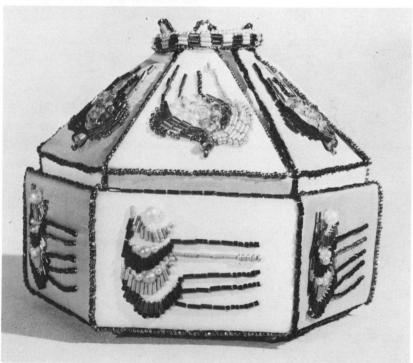

Beadwork box
Honor Costello

PLATE VII

Appliqué   Olive Smith

Introduction

We hear a great deal today about the value of using a limited number of colours in a piece of embroidery. It is a sound idea, which, when followed, usually results in work which looks both charming and elegant. Restraint is the key word for all those who aspire to produce works of art. It is equally important to limit the number of stitches and, in so doing, to extract the maximum value and variety from each one. In *Needlework through the Ages* by Mary Symonds and Louisa Preece, there is a sentence which reads 'It should be remembered that it is not the stitch itself, but *the manner of its use* which constitutes the art of embroidery'. I have always acknowledged the truth of this, and feel that once a stitch has been mastered it is necessary to discover both its possibilities and its limitations before passing on to another one. So often a stitch which appears to be useful for nothing except a rather dull straight line, suddenly blossoms during the course of an experiment into something which is versatile and extremely beautiful. Indeed it is a most rewarding exercise to embroider a whole piece of work with variations of one stitch, with one colour and one kind of thread. Textures and differences of tone come about by the skilful use of the chosen stitch.

One often meets a wall of resistance when one suggests that it is not always necessary to work a stitch exactly as it is shown in a diagram. This resistance generally springs from the fear of doing the wrong thing, and I have found that it does take courage and perseverance to fly in the face of tradition. Recently a friend of mine said that she felt really daring when she chose from a list of powdering in an embroidery book *tête-de-bœuf* as a filling for a shape she was working on a net curtain. She was amazed by the beauty of the stitch which, until then, she had believed to be suitable only for a closely woven fabric.

There is a rather stiff and unbending attitude towards traditional methods which almost excludes any attempt at an original approach. This is a greaty pity, because ideas which seem bizarre when they are first suggested gradually become accepted, and even traditional, in the course of time. Naturally not all new ideas are good, or even workable, but without experiments the good as well as the bad are stillborn. Many years ago a student of mine exhibited a piece of work in a competition, which, to her astonishment, was disqualified simply because it differed from tradition in a very mild way. Today her method would not cause a single eyebrow to be raised.

This leads me to explain that the object of this book is to encourage people to dare to be different. I hasten to add that I have no time for the deliberately poor technique which is so often presented as a gesture of defiance at tradition, worked, one is solemnly assured, in the cause of freedom and self expression. I have no time for ill mounted or soiled work, and very little for embroidery, no matter how original, which is totally unsuitable for its purpose. Neither have I a great deal of sympathy for the experienced and clever needlewomen who are so narrow in their outlook that they condemn every serious effort to widen and enrich the field of embroidery. Since no one person can possibly know all the answers, the last word will never be said. That is why we must encourage those who are eager to venture along new paths, seeking technical proficiency and original ideas as they go.

Diagrams, however clear and simple they appear to be to the person who made them, often mislead and confuse the earnest and skilful worker. A short time ago I visited a really experienced group of embroiderers, and one of them said she would be glad to see couched fillings and other stitches drawn in a variety of shapes. They are generally shown in little squares, and the average reader, she said, is apt to think that there the matter ends. In order to try to make amends for this lack of sympathy and understanding on my part, the stitches which are to be found in this book have been drawn first as line stitches (for clearness and because it is easier to work a new stitch on a straight line) and then developed as fillings for simple shapes. It is hoped that these arrangements will suggest many more ideas to those who find great pleasure in experimenting.

Some of the traditional methods are often condemned as mechanical, too laborious and too tight, and therefore quite unsuitable for the person who has a modern approach to needlecraft. This is quite untrue, as I have discovered after years of feeling impatient with the apparent lack of possibilities for development in many old varieties of embroidery. Indeed I have reached the stage where I feel that stitches and methods alone will give the embroiderer all the effects she requires, and I am not now inclined to make use of aids such as walnut shells and pieces of broken glass. Hence ideas for giving a new look to the old and well tried methods follow the stitch diagrams. Some of the ideas are still in the experimental stage, but others have proved their worth on many occasions.

The revolution in our approach to domestic and ecclesiastical embroidery which has been taking place since pre-World War II days, was absolutely necessary. It has resulted in many fine pieces of work which do speak in the idiom of the twentieth century, and are worthy to be preserved for posterity. Yet in spite of all this shaking up, this re-creation of an art which almost died of boredom, I feel strongly that pure stitchery has been neglected far too long. Therefore I make no apology for defending the cause of those (myself included) who feel happiest when they are striving to create yet another piece of original needlecraft.

1 Versatile Stitches

There is no stitch which cannot be used in a multitude of ways, and each way has several characteristics which depend upon the background, the embroidery thread and the scale of the piece of work. It is quite impossible to show in diagrams the full range of the effects and possibilities of stitches. One can only suggest ideas and hope that they will lead the reader on to experiment for herself.

The scale of the work often determines the thickness of the thread, but do remember that this rule does not always apply. Some coarse threads look lovely on very fine fabrics, and conversely a spidery effect on a heavy fabric is sometimes desirable.

Always analyse a stitch carefully, and do not forget to study the back of it. Some stitches are reversible, some are effective on both sides, and most stitches are decorative enough to be used on transparent fabrics even when crossing threads are visible on the right side. Indeed the misty shadow of threads on the wrong side of the work often enhances the right side. The wrong side of stitches can be decorated with whipping and threading and made to look very important, which is often necessary when the embroidery is to be used as a curtain, a room divider or an evening stole.

A

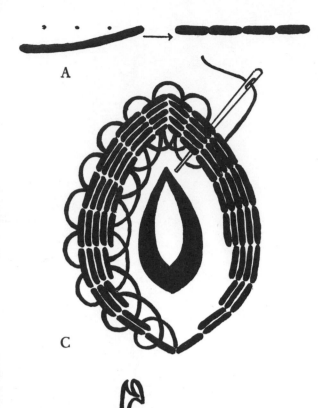

C

B

1 Diminishing Pekinese Begin with a row of back stitch, A. Work several rows close together, each a little shorter than the last, B. Lace these rows with a coarse, soft thread as for pekinese stitch. Try this method for outlining any shape, for example the leaf which is shown at C. Begin to lace the back stitches from the bottom of the shape, and make the loops as long or as short as desired. I prefer short loops, especially on household linen, because short loops give a crisp effect and they are not affected by laundering. Note that in the centre of the leaf the arrangement of the back stitches is reversed.

D shows a pear shape worked with another arrangement of diminishing pekinese. This method is much prettier than it appears to be, and it can be developed in numerous ways. Note how the lengths of the rows of back stitch vary. Try the effect of graduated tones of one colour for the back stitch, laced with a sharply contrasting tone or colour. Or use a dull, fine thread for the back stitch, and a lustrous thick silk for the lacing, both of the same colour.

A lacy effect is shown at E, where a space is left between the rows of back stitch. Note that the rows are irregular in length at both ends.

Begin here

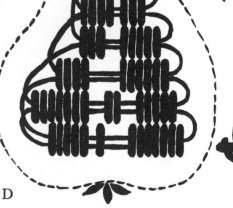

D

E

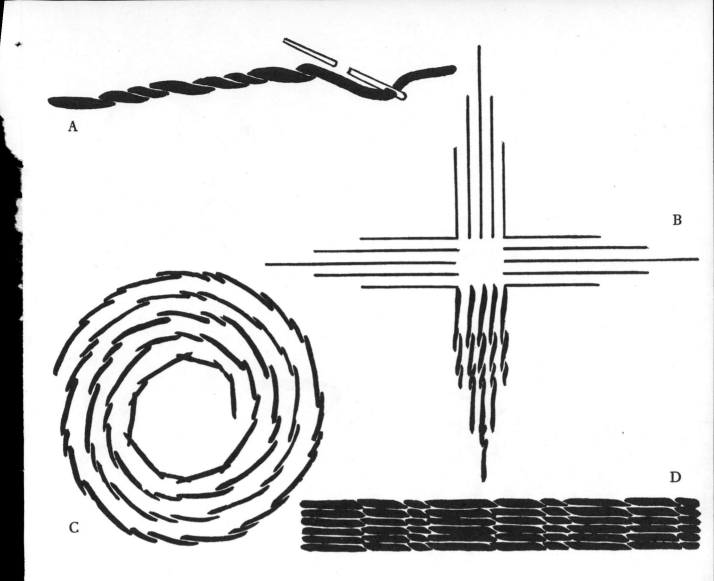

A

B

C

D

2 *Triple Stem* The wrong side of back stitch gives us another well known stitch, which is generally called *stem*. The easiest way to alter the appearance of stem is to vary the size of the stitches in a pre-arranged and regular sequence. In diagram A the order is long, medium, short, long, medium, short, repeated as often as necessary.

B shows a simple cross, the arms of which are embroidered with five rows, unequal in length, of triple stem. Each row begins in the centre of the cross.

C shows a catherine wheel which is worked spirally.

D shows several rows worked very close together as a filling. It can be used for either straight or curved shapes.

From stem stitch it is easy to progress to herringbone, which is one of our most useful stitches. It is both decorative and functional, and there seems to be no end to its variations. In shadow work, appliqué, insertion, drawn ground, drawn thread, shi-sha and canvas work it often plays a major part. It is used in smocking, plain needlework and numerous kinds of surface work. Now we add three-dimensional effects and fillings for all kinds of shapes, to prove that it is still possible to discover new ways of using this remarkable stitch.

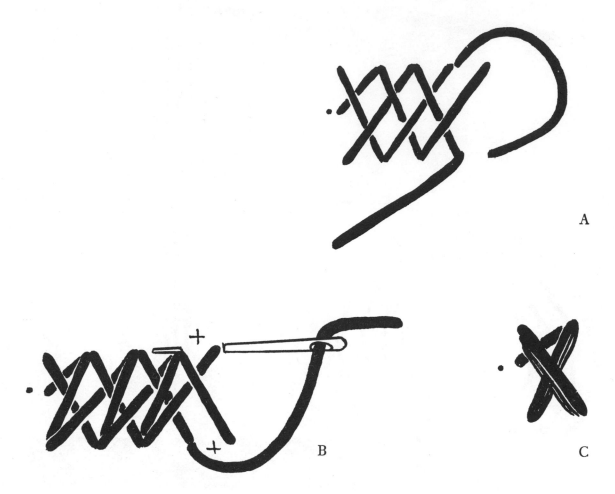

A

B

C

3 *Heavy Herringbone* Work a row of closed herringbone as shown at A, and having mastered the simple form, begin again and make a raised line by working each stitch three times in the same place before passing to the next one, B. Single stitches, as at C, can be used alone, or as a powdering. The stitch may be worked more than 3 times if a really raised effect is needed.
D shows the same stitch arranged to fill a closed diamond.
E shows a larger, open diamond.
F shows a zig-zag line. To obtain this effect repeat the first and second movements of D alternately.

D

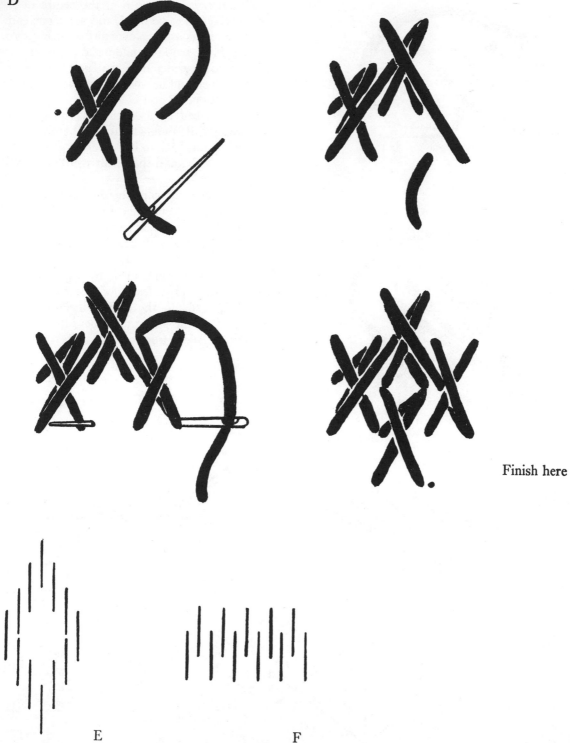

Finish here

E F

17

A

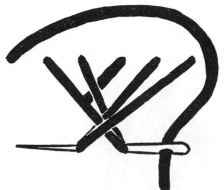

B

4 *Fan Herringbone* Begin at the centre of the shape which is to be filled, and make one complete stitch, as at A. Now work as many more stitches as are required, and make the upper part of each stitch wider than the last. The base of each stitch should be worked into the same place as the first one, B and C.

This stitch can be used to make all kinds of interesting little units and formal borders.

D Place 2 fans back to back, add fly stitches for head and body, and the result will be a simple butterfly.

E To make a diamond border work the fans alternately face to face and back to back.

F For a leaf shape make the centre stitch very tall, then gradually decrease the height of the succeeding stitches.

G A little flying fish is made by beginning with the shortest and widest stitch, as shown at 1. Work upwards to the desired height, and if necessary tie the last stitch where it crosses at the top, 2. Add a french knot for the eye.

C

D

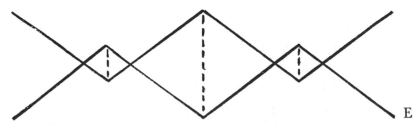

E

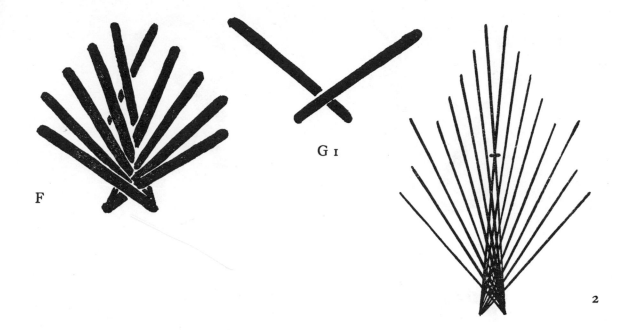

F   G 1   2

5 Overlaid Herringbone is a development of simple herringbone, and there are 2 variations. See A, B and C.

A Work at least 3 times over the first stitch, taking the same piece of fabric for the base of each layer and moving slightly upwards at the top of each stitch, until the required height and thickness is obtained. Work a row in this manner.

B Make a complete herringbone stitch, then work another one, the top of which should encircle the first, but its base must be worked a little to the right. Now make a third stitch in a similar manner. This completes stitch one. Move right and work another complete stitch, then overlay it twice. Repeat to the end of the row. This stitch looks interesting when it is used on a curved line.

C is a variation of B. Note how the top of each overlay is widened on the right side. When all these line stitches can be worked easily, return to A and try some simple fillings.

D shows a single unit, which makes an interesting powdering. This is a useful stitch for experimental work, since it can be raised to any height

by repeating the overlays as necessary. When wear and tear have to be considered, it is a good idea to tie the top of the last overlay for extra security.

E Four units arranged as a cross would look charming on church linen.

F is the basis for a snowflake. Add extra stitchery to complete the unit.

G is a 5-pointed star.

Variations of B

H Four single units, each overlaid 3 times and placed top to top, makes a swastika.

I Work 2 units corner to corner and overlay each 4 times, for a shape which resembles a pair of wings.

J A neat oblong is formed by units which are overlaid 4 times. Remember to reverse the units on each short side of the oblong.

K To make a hexagon work 4 units as for the oblong, but increase the depth of the stitches in each unit to make the 4 short sides.

L Reminds one of wind blowing through the branches of a tree. Overlay each unit 4 times and group the units in pairs.

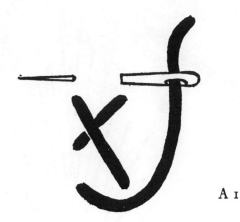

A 1

2

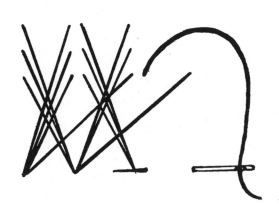

3

4

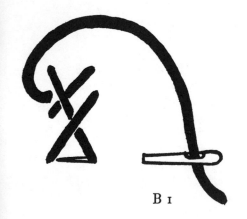

B 1

2

20

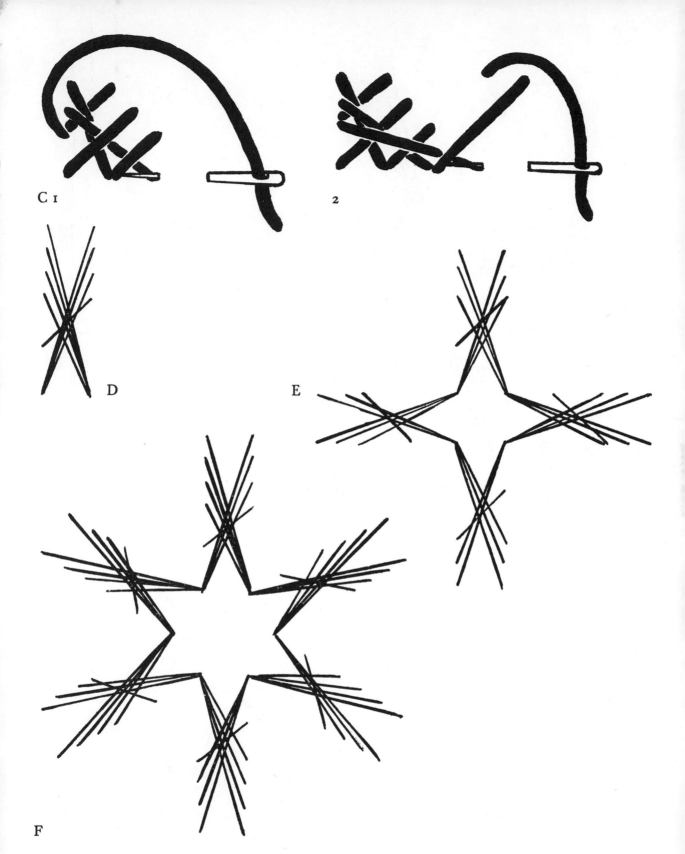

C 1

2

D

E

F

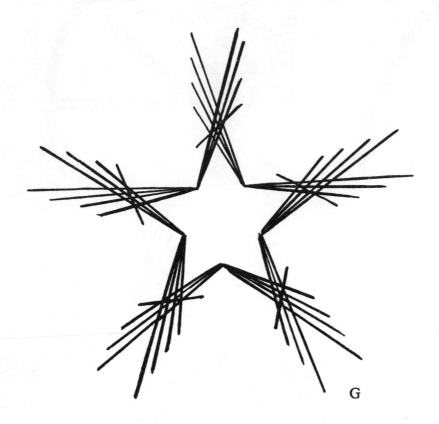

G

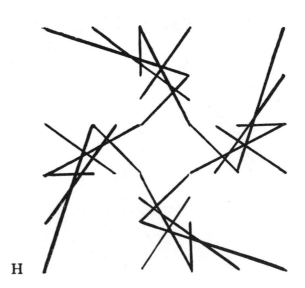

H

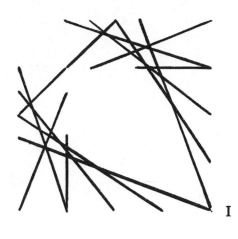
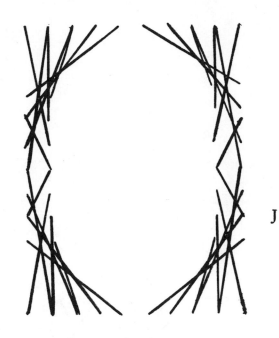

I

J

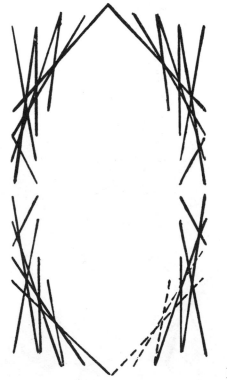
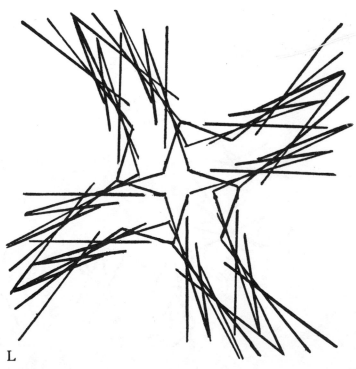

K L

23

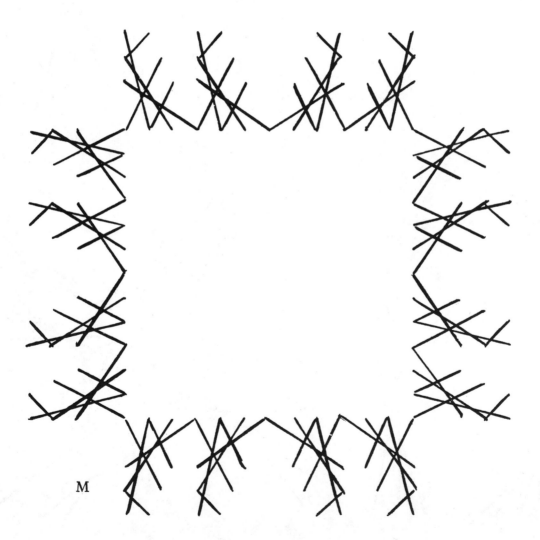

M

Variations of C

M shows a simple way in which to outline a
square. Work 4 units in reversed pairs on each
side of the shape.

N *Framed herringbone* is composed of 4 units in
reversed pairs.

O *Saltire* Place 4 units back to back and reversed.

P *Triangle* is composed of 2 units placed back to
back.

Q *Diamond* Place 4 units back to back and end
to end.

R *Fret* Note carefully how the last unit is linked
to the first one.

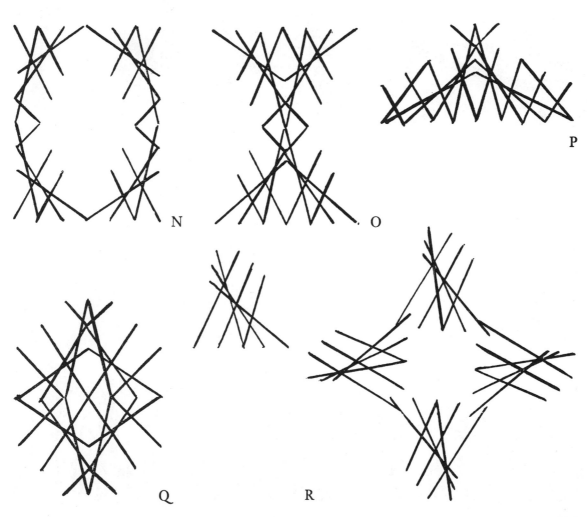

6A *Double Herringbone* Work I complete herringbone stitch, then work another shorter one over it. Repeat.

B is a variation in which the stitches are splayed. Both of these stitches look very attractive when they are worked right over narrow bands of appliqué. The bands need not be regular in shape. It follows that small areas such as petal shapes can be filled easily in this manner.

C shows a spot filled with double herringbone. Begin at the left in the centre of the circumference of the circle, and gradually increase and then decrease the size of the stitches in order to fill the shape completely. The size of the spot will probably govern the thickness of the thread. It does depend ultimately on the effect which is required.

D shows a semi-circle. Follow the upper curve carefully and work the lower part of the stitches on the straight line.

E *Triangle* Begin at the left where the stitches will be large enough to work easily, and then gradually decrease the height of the stitches as the shape becomes narrower.

F *Oval* Begin at the left and work carefully across the shape.

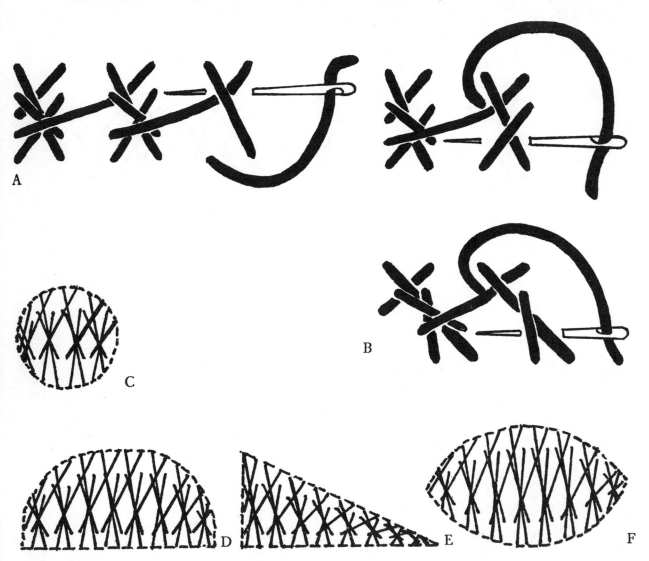

A

B

C

D

E

F

26

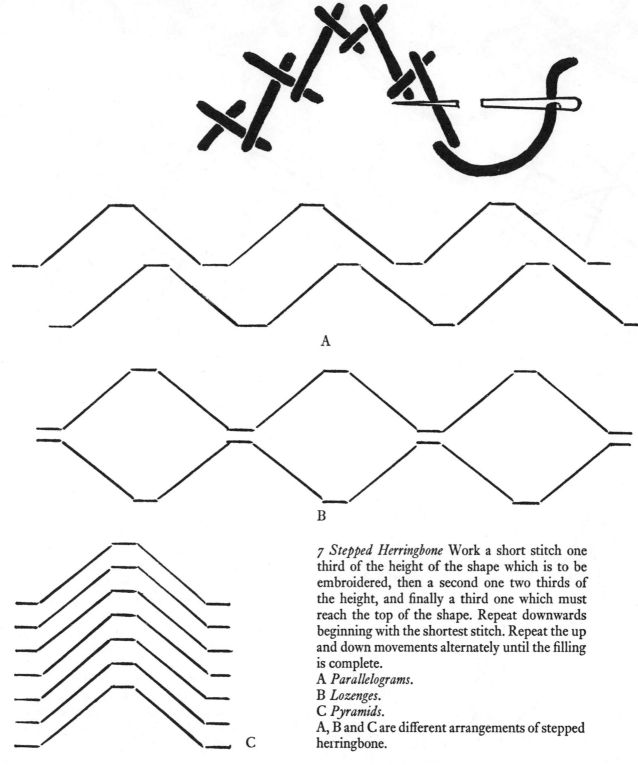

A

B

C

7 Stepped Herringbone Work a short stitch one third of the height of the shape which is to be embroidered, then a second one two thirds of the height, and finally a third one which must reach the top of the shape. Repeat downwards beginning with the shortest stitch. Repeat the up and down movements alternately until the filling is complete.

A *Parallelograms.*

B *Lozenges.*

C *Pyramids.*

A, B and C are different arrangements of stepped herringbone.

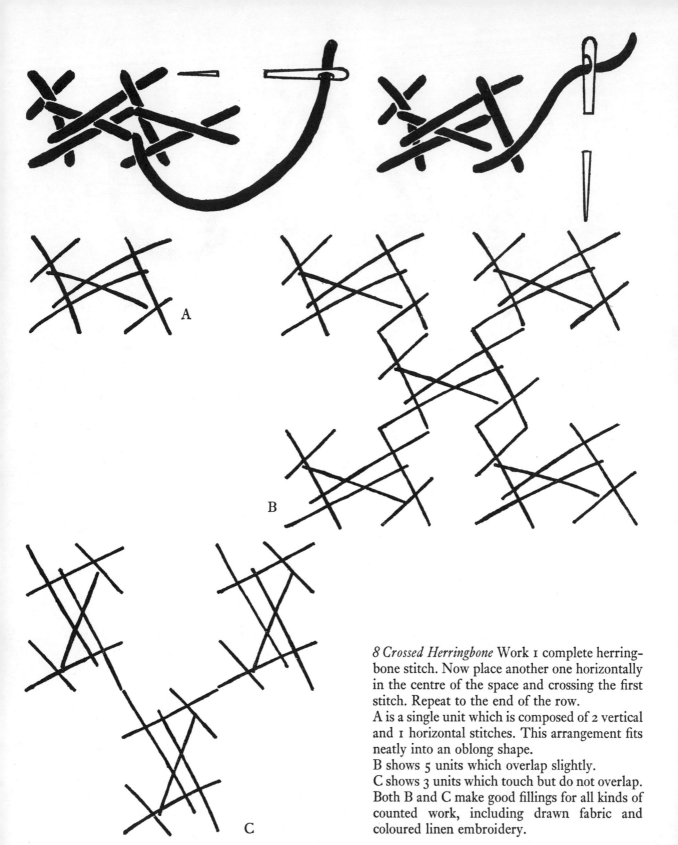

8 Crossed Herringbone Work 1 complete herring-bone stitch. Now place another one horizontally in the centre of the space and crossing the first stitch. Repeat to the end of the row.

A is a single unit which is composed of 2 vertical and 1 horizontal stitches. This arrangement fits neatly into an oblong shape.

B shows 5 units which overlap slightly.

C shows 3 units which touch but do not overlap. Both B and C make good fillings for all kinds of counted work, including drawn fabric and coloured linen embroidery.

9 Simple Couching is very easy to do and it can be worked on all kinds of fabric. The best results are obtained when the ground fabric is held quite taut in a frame, so that the left hand is free to guide the thread.

A shows an interesting pentagon, which is quite simple to draw, but it can be tacked upon the ground if necessary. Tack or trace a cross with arms of equal length, and from the ends of the horizontals tack straight lines to the base. Join the tips of the horizontals to the top of the upper arm. Divide each side line into equal parts and make the same number of equal divisions on the upper arm.

B Couch pale toned threads from the dots on each line.

C Couch dark toned horizontal lines from side to side and over the pale couching.

Note the arrangement of the couching stitches, as it is important to place them properly.

D *Double Pentagon* Mark out the figure carefully.

E Work all the diagonal rows of couching first with a light coloured thread. Add dark, horizontal rows to complete the figure, and place the couching stitches carefully. This shape can be extended indefinitely and made into large shapes and border patterns.

F *Inside, outside* Mark the figure as shown in the diagram.

G Couch the upper horizontals first, and then the lower ones. It is possible to make all kinds of colour variations with these figures, and to re-arrange the sequence of the couched lines.

No doubt it will have been noticed that all the 3 figures could be worked in English or corded quilting. *Do* experiment with them.

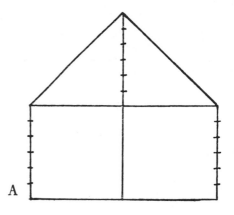

A

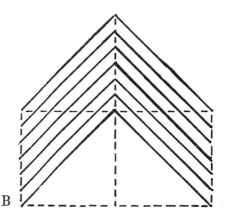

B

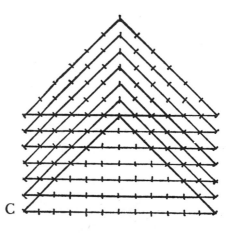

C

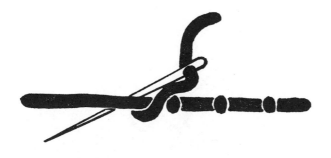

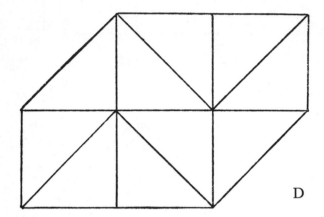

D

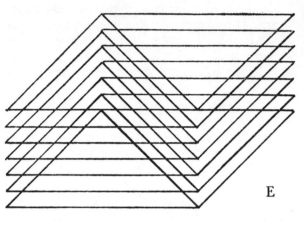

E

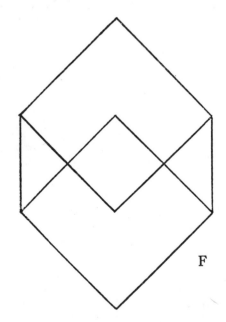

F

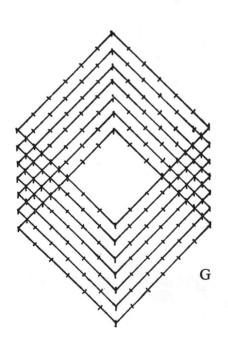

G

10 Looped Chevron is decorative and it can be worked with coarse or fine threads in numerous ways. There are 3 movements for each stitch.

A shows looped chevron used as an insertion stitch.

B This filling looks interesting either on a closely woven fabric or on openly woven linen. If it is worked fairly tightly it becomes a drawn ground stitch.

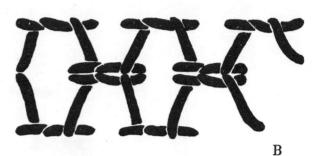

B

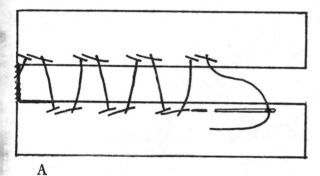

A

11 Alternating Chevron is useful for a variety of fillings. Note that the base of the stitch is twice as wide as the top.

A shows a broad border which can be developed into a filling by working several rows close together.

A

B is a small diamond. Note the arrangement of the short 'feet'.

C is a large diamond. Note how the stitches are reversed in the second half of the filling.

D is an enclosed block, which can be of any size and almost any shape. Simply close the block with running stitches worked between the chevron stitches on the outer edges of the shape.

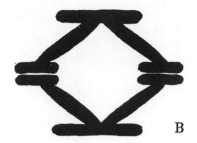

B

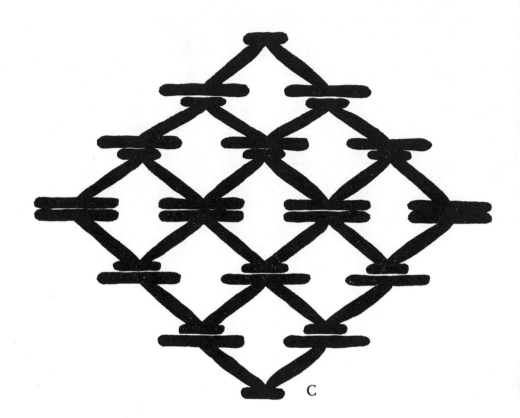

C

D

12 Spaced Chevron Make the first piece of the
'foot' half as long as the second piece. Use this
stitch for lines and borders and fillings.

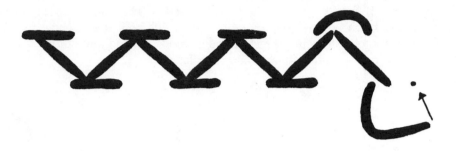

13 Overlapped Chevron Work 1 'foot' on the
upper edge of a border, and another on the
lower edge. Now make a third 'foot' in the
centre of the border which overlaps the long
thread between the upper and lower stitches.
Move to the top and repeat to the end of the row.
This stitch is very interesting on the back, and it
is especially useful for embroidery on net and
other transparent fabrics.
It can be used for attaching appliqué to its
ground, or developed into a filling stitch.

14 Pylon Chevron Gradually increase the height of the stitches as far as desired, then drop to the height of the smallest stitch and begin again. There is really no limit to the number of variations of this stitch.

A Draw a leaf shape and mark the central vein. Begin at the bottom left and work to the top of the leaf, then turn and work downwards on the right side. If the filling seems loose (either because the stitch is too wide, or the thread too fine) work another row in the middle and on top of the first row. Alternatively couch the long threads with one or two stitches each.

B *Triangles* Place 2 right angled triangles back to back to make an arrow head. Add more, but smaller triangles if it is necessary to lengthen the shape. Begin to work at the widest end of the shapes, and note that there are 2 rows of stitching in each arrow head.

C *Reversed Triangles* make an interesting border. The loose loops in the diagram show how to pass from one triangle to another. They should be pulled quite tight.

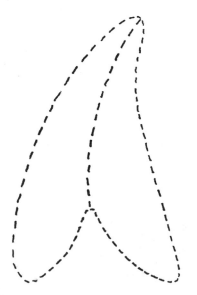

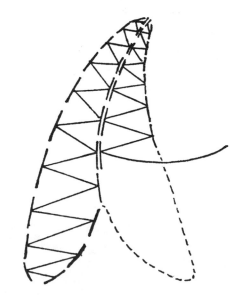

A

34

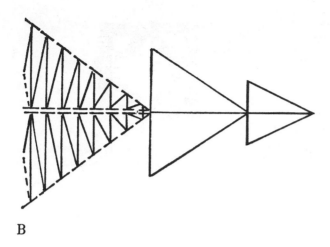

B

C

15 Squared Chevron makes a pretty line stitch. Begin on the left side of the lower edge of the border, and work one 'foot'. Continue working in a clockwise movement until the square is complete. Take the thread under the middle of the first 'foot' and then out on the right lower edge ready for the next square.

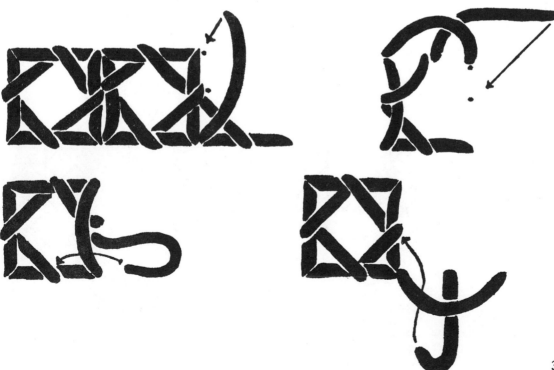

A *Detached Square* One unit can be used alone, or powdered over an area to make a light filling.
B *Blocks* Arrange rows of overlapping units to form any required shape.
C *Quadrate* Rows of blocks arranged to form a solid figure.
D *St Chad* This cross of Saint Chad could be worked with white thread on church linen.
E *Stepped Cross* shows another arrangement of blocks of squared chevron which could be used for ecclesiastical embroidery.

A

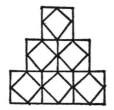

B

C

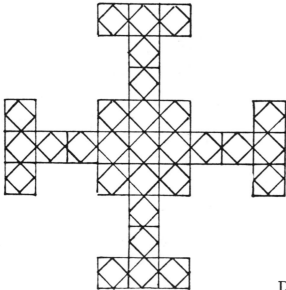

D

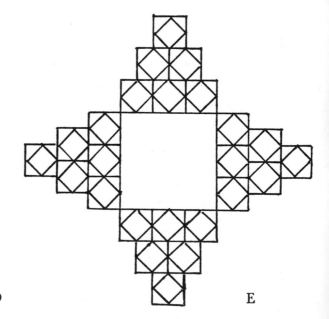

E

Since leaves are so beautiful and come in such a diversity of shapes, they are deservedly popular with embroiderers. The following 6 ways for filling leaf shapes with adaptations of line stitches should help readers to discover other methods for themselves.

16 Star Herringbone Work 2 complete herringbone stitches, then tie them in the centre as shown in the diagram. Move to the top of the border and repeat.

17 This flat leaf shape looks charming when it is filled with one row of star herringbone. Draw the leaf on the fabric and mark the centre vein. Begin at the left, and in order to avoid muddle, carefully work 2 pairs of herringbone in each half of the leaf. Elongate the stitches where necessary so that they follow the outline accurately. Add any other enrichment which is felt to be required.

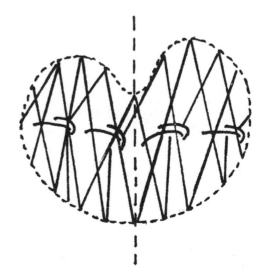

18 This heart shaped leaf is filled with double herringbone, which is shown at 6A. Mark the centre vein and, beginning at the top each time, work each half separately.

19 Elongated Wheatear Begin in the centre of the border and work 3 satin stitches on each side. Note that the middle stitches are longer than the outer ones. Move 1 stitch length down the line and work 2 pairs of satin stitches. From the base of these pairs move upwards and work a long pair to link the first group with the second. Continue to the end of the line.

20 Draw a leaf shape, and add 3 vertical veins, a straight centre one and a curved one on each side of it. Begin at the top and work each half separately.

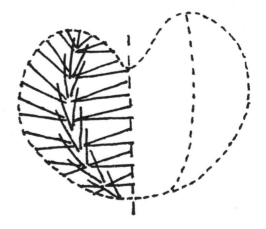

21 Alternating Wheatear Note that there are 3
satin stitches, then 1, alternately down the row.
The rest of the working is the same as for simple
wheatear.

22 Draw a leaf and mark the centre vein. Divide
each lobe in half with a curved line. Begin at the
bottom of each lobe and work with alternating
wheatear, splaying the stitches to fit the shape.

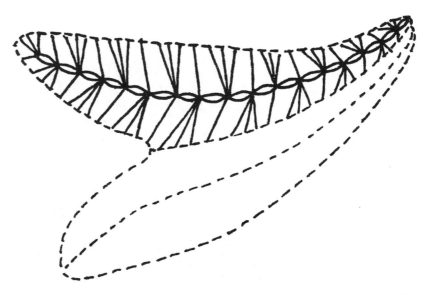

23 Fringed Buttonhole Work a pair of upright buttonhole stitches very close together, then link them with a chain stitch. Work another pair of chained buttonhole stitches upside down. Now work a pair horizontally which pass over the first pair. Repeat from the beginning. This is a very pretty line stitch which looks effective on curved edges, such as necklines of dresses.

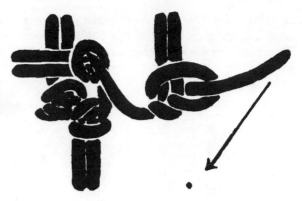

24 Draw a leaf and divide it into 4 equal portions. Begin at the bottom of each lobe and work so that the heavy side of the stitch is on the edge of the leaf.

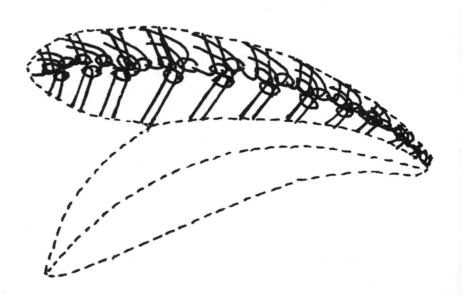

40

25 Triple Crossed Buttonhole Work a diagonal buttonhole from right to left. Embroider 3 buttonhole stitches facing left to right over the first stitch. Note that the stitches in the group of 3 gradually increase in height, and that the last one is as long as the first single stitch. Repeat.

26 Draw a heart shaped leaf and add a central vein. Begin at the top and work each half separately.

Beads and sequins are a challenge to the imaginative embroiderer. She does not always wish to make her work too glittery, and yet the beautiful effect of sparkling sequins cannot be denied. If beads and sequins are attached with decorative stitchery which partly conceals them, the effect is both restrained and chunky. Remember that wooden beads, pierced discs of wood or plastic, Indian mirrors (shi-sha glass) and many other items are included in this work.

27 Indian mirrors can be held in place with squared chevron. So can sequins if one fills the centre hole with small beads. I find it best to fix the mirror in position with the smallest smear of paste before adding the stitches.

Large sequins with a big hole in them can be attached in many interesting ways, as quite thick embroidery threads pass easily through them.

28 Work radiating lines of threaded or whipped back stitch on the top edge only.

29 Couch short lines across the top edge of the sequin, and work a block of needleweaving on radiating threads over the lower piece. Take care to use a sufficiently long piece of thread for the weaving, as it is almost impossible to make a neat join through a sequin.

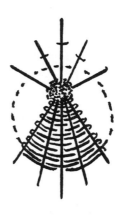

30 Herringbone, overlaid in the hole and splayed at the top looks quite effective, especially if small beads are added between the stitches.
Small sequins lend themselves to many decorative arrangements, and they always seem to be more interesting when half hidden with stitchery.

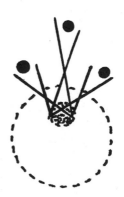

31 Shows a row of sequins held in position with fly stitch.

32 A group of 4 sequins held in place with radiating satin stitches.

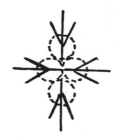

33 Five sequins held with radiating satin stitches arranged like a saltire cross.

34 Nine sequins held with satin stitches and detached chain.

 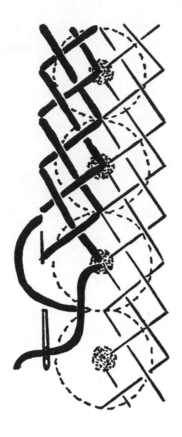 

35 Sequins held with a form of wheatear. Large or small sequins, and flat beads with a central hole can be attached with many varieties of wheatear.

36 Large sequins make a lacy border if they are attached with 2 rows of herringbone. As a further enrichment beads, either round or bugle, may be added to the herringbone stitch.

37 Sequins attached with back stitch can be made even more interesting by adding various forms of pekinese threading.

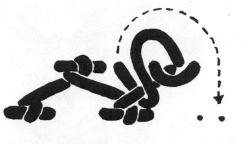

38 Twisted Chevron Complete 1 'foot', then lace the thread round the long stitch before making the second 'foot'. See A and B.
Add bugles to alternate long stitches as shown at C.

A

B

C

39 Long Legged Chevron Simply close up the stitches and the central threads will become alternately diagonal and straight. A.
Add beads to the diagonal threads. B.

A

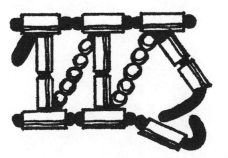

B

45

40 Winged Wheatear Arrange fanned groups of satin stitches at each side of a central line, then move 1 stitch length downwards and lace under the right fan only. A.

Add beads to the left side of the lacing. B.

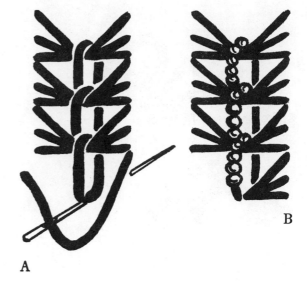

A

B

41 Blocked Wheatear On the left side of a central line work 1 chain stitch, and carry the thread upwards on the right side. Move 1 stitch length downwards and lace under the short stitch and the top edge only of the chain. Work 4 stitches in this manner and then reverse, placing the chain stitches on the opposite side. Repeat the left and right blocks alternately. A.

Add a flat little bead to the tails of the chain stitches. B.

A

B

46

42 _Tied Wheatear_ Work 3 pairs of satin stitches, each pair slightly lower than the last. Move 1 stitch length below the last pair and then take the thread over and under the stitches on the left. Next work under and over the stitches on the right, pass the needle under the thread and into the centre, where it will be ready for the next group of satin stitches. A.

Add beads to the cross bar. B.

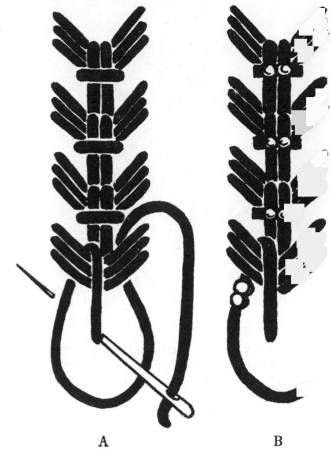

A   B

43 _Fanned Wheatear_ Work 3 splayed satin stitches on the left. Move down, level with the outer end of the last stitch. Now work 3 more splayed satin stitches as follows:

1 Should reach as high as the first stitch in the previous group.
2 Should be as high as the second one.
3 Should be horizontal.

Move down 1 stitch length and thread under both groups before returning the needle to the centre. Repeat from the beginning. A.

Add bugle beads to the 3 stitches on the left, and to the first one on the right. B.

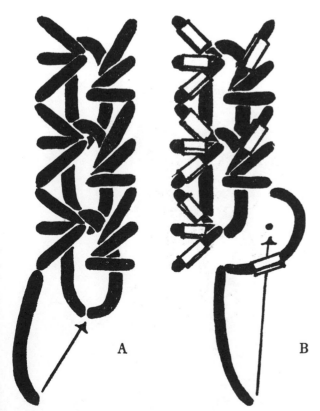

A   B

47

A

B

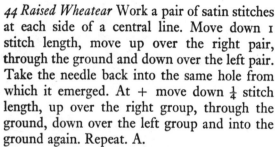

44 Raised Wheatear Work a pair of satin stitches at each side of a central line. Move down 1 stitch length, move up over the right pair, through the ground and down over the left pair. Take the needle back into the same hole from which it emerged. At + move down ¼ stitch length, up over the right group, through the ground, down over the left group and into the ground again. Repeat. A.

Place bugles on the last pair of upright stitches. B.

45 Chained Wheatear Work a diagonal chain on the left, and another one facing upwards on the right. Move down 1 stitch length and link the top edges of the chain only. Repeat. A.

Thread beads on the sides of the chains. B.

A

B

46 Beads on Stem Stitch On each of 5 stem stitches thread 1 bead, then work 4 stitches without a bead. Repeat beads and plain stitches alternately.

47 Beads on Tied Herringbone With coarse threads use oval wooden beads or big glass ones, and with fine threads use bugles or smallish round glass beads. Tie the herringbone either with a stitch or several small beads threaded on silk.

48 Fly Stitch and Beads The diagram shows a simple form which is easy to follow. Try other variations of fly stitch.

49 Feather Stitch with Beads Experiment with beads of different sizes and shapes, and, of course, with variations of feather stitch.

50 Buttonhole with Beads Note the varied height of the stitches. There are many kinds of buttonhole stitch and it will prove very rewarding to experiment with them all.

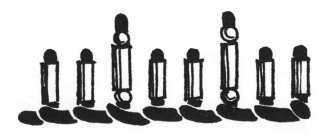

2 *Squaring the Circle*

Many of the lovely things which excite the imagination, and make an embroiderer long to get out her sewing materials, are based on a circle. Flowers, shells, soap bubbles, whirlpools and wells can be suggested simply and pleasingly with stitches. Try ideas on paper first. Draw round lids, thimbles and any circular object of the required size, and then scribble ideas for the division of larger circles. Move from scribbles on paper to scribbles with stitches on a piece of material. Gradually it will be found that in order to interpret the scribbles in a lively manner, it will be necessary to devise new ways of working stitches which have been known for generations. Good ideas should be enlarged, and developed into complete articles like mats and cushion covers, stool tops and boxes. It is so easy if the beginnings are small, because most people feel capable of managing a small shape, whereas large shapes are rather intimidating. Use plates, cups and wine glasses for large circles, as our ancestors did when quilting, and remember that in a very large shape some alteration in the stitching will be necessary. A few enlarged ideas will be found ideal for quilting, appliqué and even for the development of patchwork, see chapter 3.

51 shows how *Threaded Running Stitch* can be given a new look. Work several rows of Run Stitch, each one a little shorter than the last, and thread with thick cotton. If desired, turn at the end and make ringed run stitch, as shown by the dotted line.

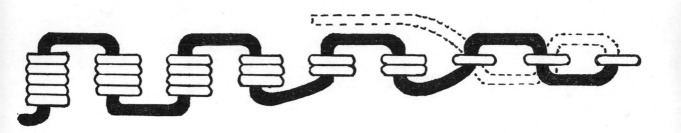

52 Circle Line The threaded run stitch, when worked round a circle, gives the illusion of an oval. Note that the stitches gradually decrease in size as the number of rows increases. Make the outer stitches rather long, to allow for this reduction. The original was worked throughout with thick thread.

53 Shell This time the same stitch is worked on a spiral, and the idea was evolved from a study of a shell. There is no need to work the design mathematically, simply draw or tack a circle on the fabric and gradually work the run stitch inwards.

54 Convolvulus This design is easy to draw with a pair of compasses. Describe a circle, and divide it as shown in the diagram. Keep the same radius, and from any point on the circumference describe an arc. Place the point of the compasses on the spot where the arc touches the circumference and draw another arc. Repeat. It will be found that 6 curved lines, each springing from the centre of the circle, will divide the shape into equal portions. If 12 portions are needed, simply find the centre between any of the points on the circumference, and repeat as before.

Doubtless many other ideas will be found, and developed, by enterprising needlewomen.

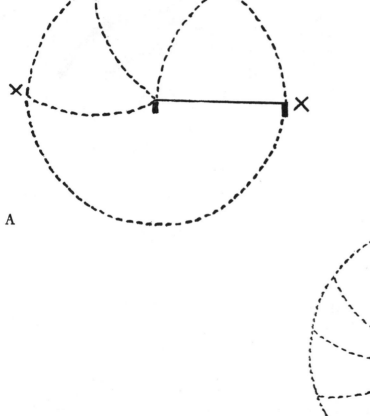

A

B

*55*A *Alternating Pekinese* From run stitch we move to back stitch. The back stitch is threaded as shown in the diagram, to make alternating pekinese stitch. Work each portion of the threading longer or shorter than its predecessor. Even alter the colour of either the threading or the back stitch, or both, at irregular intervals.

*55*B *Split Rings* Alternating pekinese is worked on concentric circles. This filling looks interesting if it is worked with back stitch which shades from a light to a dark tone on each circle. The threading should be of 1 colour only, and slightly thicker than the back stitch.

It is not necessary to thread all the way round each circle, as breaks in the line are interesting.

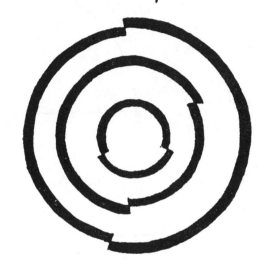

*56*A *Alternate Back* The interesting method of whipping gives our old friend back stitch a new look. Work the whipping firmly. The stitches in the diagram are shown loose for the sake of clarity. Use it for the next idea.

Row 1

Row 2

56B Bubbles This idea was suggested by soap bubbles. Within a circle draw several overlapping ones, using a thimble, coins and so forth, if compasses are not available. Work each circle with different weights of thread of the same colour, beginning with fine threads for the larger circles and ending with coarse threads for the small ones. This filling is easy to vary. Do experiment.

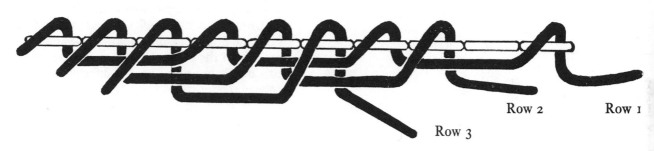

Row 2   Row 1

Row 3

57A Triple Back Stitch It is easy to follow the diagram. Work the threading quite firmly with 3 different colours, or 1, as desired. This stitch makes a firm, thick line which is slightly raised. Use it for the next idea.

The crosses mark the centres of the circles.

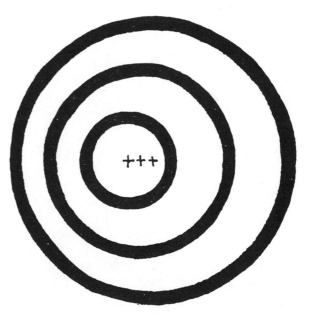

57B Spinning Top Several colours are required to give the illusion of movement. Watch a child's top and vary this theme.

55

58A *Threaded Loop* This method was discovered on an old piece of shadow work, which was probably embroidered at the beginning of this century. Instead of the back stitches making a firm line round the shape, each one was left as a small loop. A slightly coarser thread than usual was used, and the loops have not pulled out of shape in spite of much laundering. Perhaps this idea was the forerunner of our candlewick embroidery. It can certainly be used for rows of back stitch, as well as double back stitch. It has possibilities also for appliqué. Leather and other materials can be lightly stuck in position, and loops worked round the applied shape. These loops should be laced with a fine thread, even with tambour. A charming filigree effect is obtained, and no stitches penetrate the appliqué. The diagram is easy to follow once it is realized that rows of double back stitch are worked behind the fabric, as for shadow work, and loops are left on the surface. A gauge such as a knitting needle is helpful, as it is difficult at first to control the length of the loops. Speed and confidence come in time, and the gauge can be discarded.

58B *Variation* shows an idea based on circles, for which this stitch is quite suitable.

59 Well An interesting effect of depth is created by working close concentric circles with any stitch. Stem was used for the original. The outer line is of very coarse thread, and each succeeding circle should be worked with a finer one than the last. One colour, or shades of one colour, beginning with the strongest one, are quite successful. Obviously a reversed effect, with the coarsest thread on the inner circle, would have to be called *dome*.

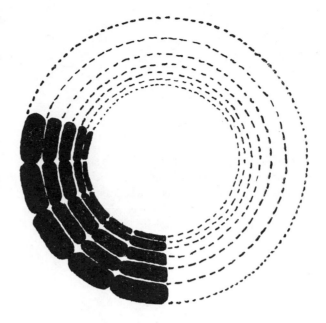

60 Dahlia 1 Work double back stitch as for shadow work, fairly loosely, taking care to work the same number of stitches on each circle. It is useful to mark each circle into even portions, say 8, before the sewing is started. Link the back stitches with herringbone worked with thread of the same weight but a different colour. From the centre, with a fine thread of the same colour as the double back stitch, work satin stitches between the herringbone stitches. Darn twice round the centre of these satin stitches for a raised effect. On the outer rim work short, fine spokes and top them with thick french knots.

61 Dahlia 2 The back of dahlia 1 is so interesting that it can be reversed and made the right side of dahlia 2. The centre is worked as for dahlia 1. On the outer edge work vee shapes with fine satin stitch.

62 Peacock

Row 1 Herringbone with a thick thread.

Row 2 Herringbone laced into row 1. The needle pierces the ground on the lower edge only.

Row 3 Mark the middle base of the circle, and work herringbone as for row 2, but practically 'mark time' with the stitches on the lower edge.

This simple foundation suggests the spread tail of a peacock, and should be adorned as required. It might be found necessary to make the herringbone firm with couching stitches placed over the intersections. Beads could be used for the 'eyes'. Try out your own ideas.

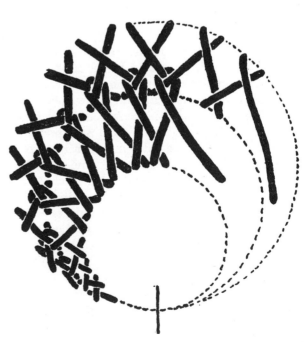

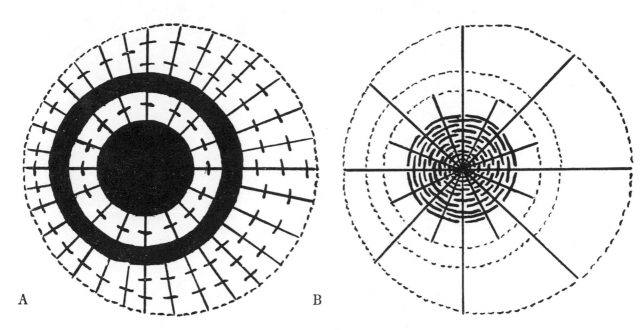

A
B

63 *Eclipse* Draw circles as shown at B, and work radiating lines with a dark thread over them, and couch these lines with long stitches, with a light thread. Weave the centre circle with dark thread. From the ends of the short, dark lines work rays with a light thread to the edge of the outer circle, and couch them. Weave the remaining bar with dark thread, as shown at A.

64 *Radiance* This filling is a development of Eclipse. Draw a circle, and from the centre work groups of radiating lines, as shown at A. Weave a wheel in the centre, and then weave each group, as shown at B. Do not pierce the ground, but turn carefully at the end of each row. When almost two thirds of the circle have been filled, weave several rows right round to make the band which is shown at A, tie the band, and add french knots. Two or more colours may be used. The original was worked with dull yellow and white threads on an ochre ground.

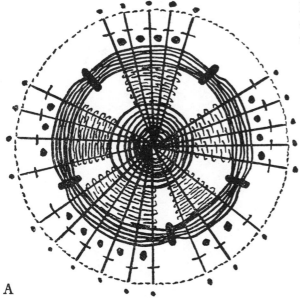

A

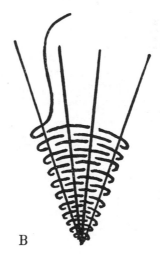

B

65 Daisy Draw 3 concentric circles, and in the first 2 work a row of vandyke buttonhole, as shown at B, and in the centre of the third one work 2 close satin stitches. With a coarse thread loop through the spaces between the top half of the buttonhole stitches and into the top satin stitch. Continue round the circle, but attach the lower half of the buttonhole stitches to the bottom satin stitch. Darn the centre with a fine thread to make a middle for the daisy, and edge it with 1 row of coarse back stitch, which should be worked round the loops and not through the ground.

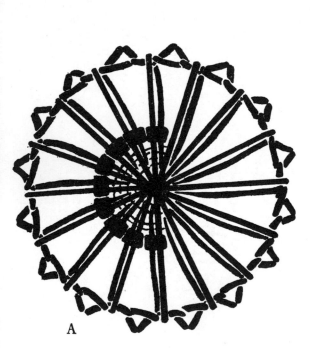

A

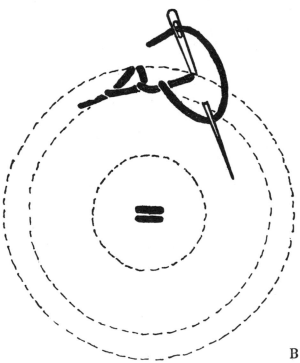

B

66 Chinese Cobweb The shape is Chinese, but the filling is really cable stitch which is used both in smocking and as a decorative centre for drawn thread borders. Place an even number of radiating satin stitches in each semi-circle, and follow the diagram for the arrangement of the satin stitch in the 'tails'. The diagram is left unfinished in order to show the spokes quite clearly. With a thicker thread work the semi-circles first, and do not pack the rows too tightly, or else the cobwebby appearance will be lost. Begin at the base of each complete semi-circle in turn, and weave to the bottom of the tail. Use a tapestry needle, and pierce the ground at the end of each row only. Work alternately from right to left and left to right, and splay the rows, as the outer curve is greater than the inner one. To add to the Chinese appearance, work one half of the filling with a light thread and the other half with a dark one.

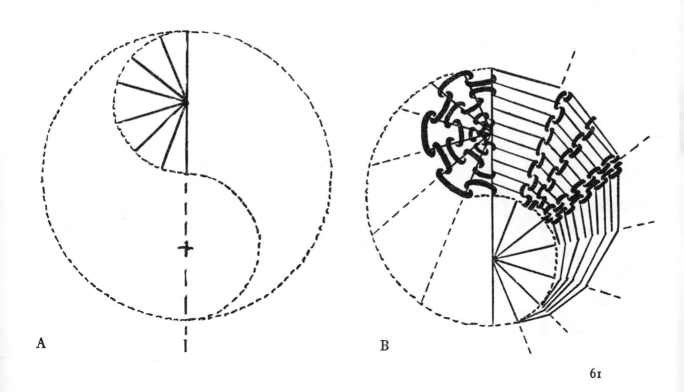

A

B

67 *Bun Case* obviously slightly creased, to give an OP effect. A shows the division of the circle, and B shows the filling. Complete both sides with coarse thread, and then couch the lines as shown at C. Note that the couching follows a spiral. Make the thick rows of couching in a contrasting colour, and the fine ones in a darker tone than the rays.

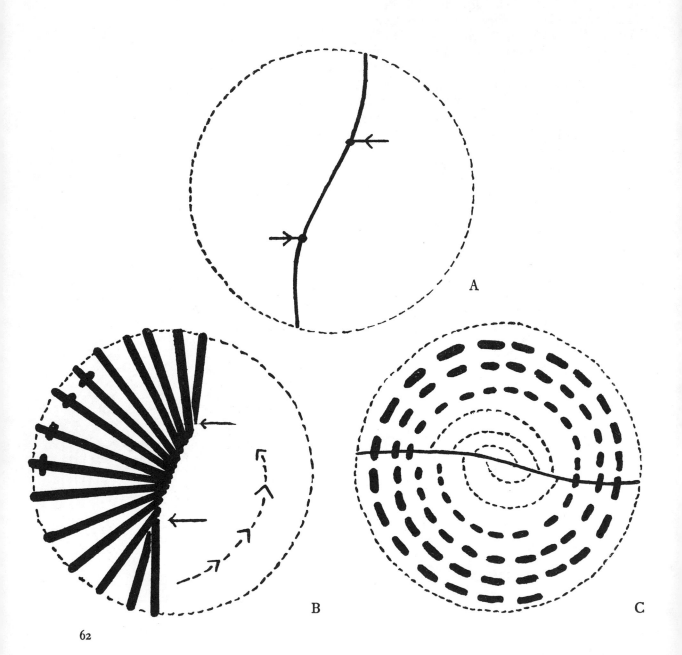

A

B

C

68 Feathers Divide the circle as shown at A, and work the lines as shown at B. Complete both feathers with the same thread in the same colour, but couch the first one with a fine matching thread, and the second one with a fine, contrasting thread.

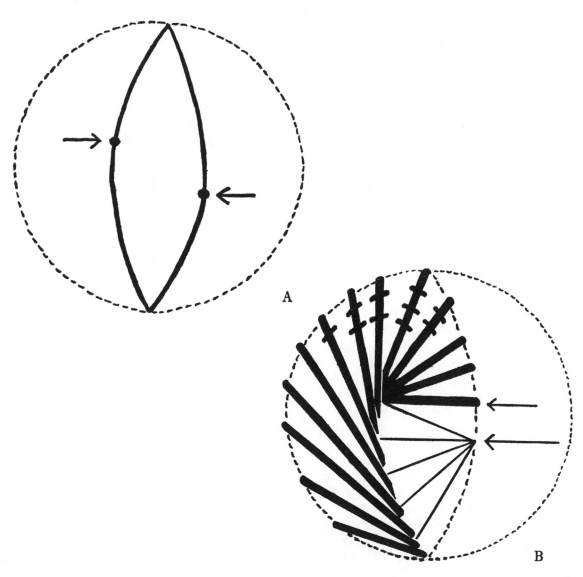

A

B

3 *Variations*

Patchwork A few experienced embroiderers, who had mastered the basic rules of patchwork, and who were capable of drawing a design and adapting it for various methods of needlecraft, decided to try to give this ancient art a new look and began to experiment. One made a very small sampler composed of tiny pieces of fine fabric, some of which measured less than half an inch when the turnings had been pressed. She discovered that it was possible to work a freely drawn design based mainly on curves if one was patient and careful. This led to further experiments. Circular pieces could be inserted quite easily into a shape if some modification of the working method was employed. Another person became eager to leave the purely experimental stage, and decided to embark upon a small piece of ecclesiastical embroidery. She began by drawing in a 9 inch square a design for a burse, based on the Pentecostal tongues of flame, and she deliberately avoided thinking in terms of patchwork. She thought instead of simple areas of colour which had a clearly defined outline, and interesting movement (Plate I). When the drawing was finished, suitable fabrics were chosen for colour and texture. It was found that very flimsy fabrics, those which frayed or stretched, and even some very tightly woven ones were quite unsuitable, but velvet, soft but heavy silk, and light weight, smooth woollen fabrics could be used with success.

Each part of the design was numbered, beginning from the bottom right corner, and then it was traced upon very thin card. The back of the card was marked with small squares, so that each piece of fabric could be cut with the grain running parallel with the edge of the design. The card was placed face upwards on a piece of glass, and carefully cut into templates with a sharp knife. As each piece was cut away it was clearly numbered on the back. The very edges of template number 1 were very lightly smeared with paste, and then it was stuck face downwards on the back of the chosen fabric, with the squares on the back matching the grain. The smear of paste was sufficient to hold the template firmly in place whilst the fabric was cut. A $\frac{1}{4}$ in. turning was allowed on all the inner edges, but where a turning was to form the outer edge of the burse, at least $\frac{1}{2}$ in. was required. The curved edges were snipped, and the corners cut away as shown in the diagram, then the edges were firmly turned over the card and secured with small tacking stitches. Each template was prepared in the same way, then, with the numbered original design as a guide, the pieces were assembled. It was not possible to over-sew them together from the back, so the pieces were connected with ladder stitch, which was worked on the right side. This stitch is invisible when it is pulled firmly, and it is possible to sew several times up and down each seam when extra security is required. The whole was fitted together like a jig-saw puzzle, but great care was needed to make an accurate 9 inch square with true corners.

When the stitching was complete, the tackings and the templates were removed, and then a matching length of bias binding was machined all round the edges to hold the seams firm and ease the problems of making up. Bulky joins were pared away with sharp scissors, and the whole was mounted on a piece of card which was padded with a sheet of thin foam rubber.

When the burse had been successfully completed, and the problems it presented had been solved, the way was paved for larger and more adventurous pieces of work of this kind.

Applied Patchwork was considered next. It was felt that there was no need to make completely solid patched shapes when they were to be applied to another piece of fabric. Several samples were created, and it was discovered that if small portions of the patchwork were omitted, a much more interesting effect was obtained. The choice of a background was very important. Good, plain ones which echoed one of the colours used in the patchwork were successful, and velvet was excellent. The pile of the velvet rose to hide the joins and also gave a gently padded appearance to the work.

69 Wrong side of card marked with small squares

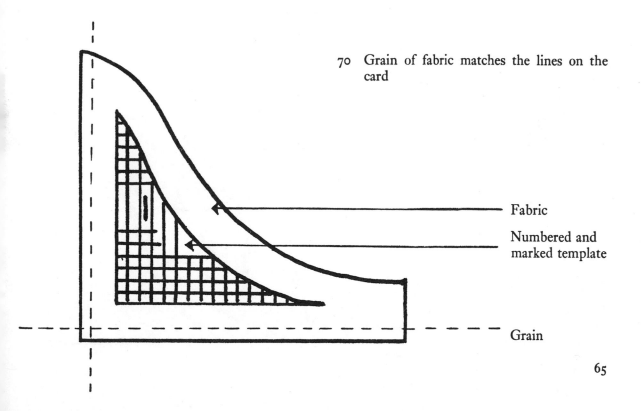

70 Grain of fabric matches the lines on the card

Fabric

Numbered and marked template

Grain

65

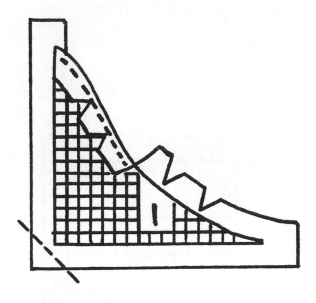

71   Mitre corners and snip curves

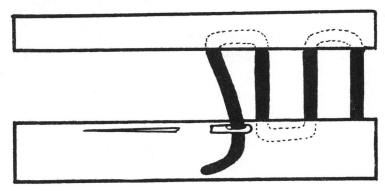

72   Ladder stitch. Pull firmly to close the gap
between the pieces of fabric

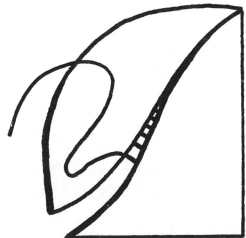

73   Ladder stitch is invisible when pulled tight.
Work on the right side

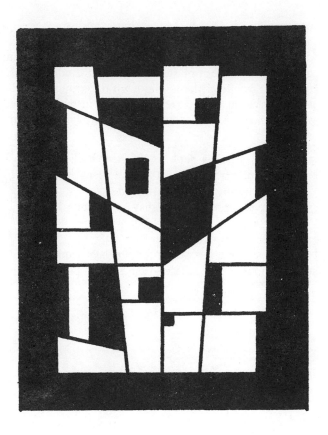

Appliqué This method has a long history and it is deservedly popular today. It gives a rich, bold colour effect which is achieved fairly quickly, and it does withstand a great deal of hard wear. Therefore it is especially suitable for work which has to be viewed from a distance, or which is used out of doors in our very unpredictable climate.

Appliqué has undergone many changes since the days when even tiny pieces of silk applied to lingerie were firmly anchored in place with hard edges of buttonhole or satin stitch. During the last decade emphasis has been placed on softening the effect, and frayed edges, slipped outlines, irregular edge stitches and cut or drawn work on the shapes themselves have all been used successfully. The illusion of movement, which is today so popular in most forms of art, has presented the embroiderer with yet another method, which is described below. The pieces which are to be applied are cut with or without a turning. If a turning is necessary it should be pressed under and tacked so that the work is easy to manage. I have found that it is a good idea to treat the pieces which need turnings like hemmed appliqué, as it is easy to keep a good shape when the fabric is tacked on paper. Remove the paper after the edges have been pressed. The pieces are placed in position, pinned, tacked and then oversewn with matching cotton. If paste will do no harm, smear the back of the appliqué lightly and press it into position before tacking. This ensures the neat professional finish which is so desirable. To oversew the edges, bring the needle to the surface just at the side of the applied shapes, and return it to the back through the smallest amount of the appliqué which is possible. Where there are no turnings it might be necessary to take a fairly long stitch, or to use herringbone instead of oversewing. Remove the tackings, and trace straight or wavy lines right across the work. (See diagram.) With threads of the same colour as the ground and as the appliqué, begin to embroider, using the colour of the appliqué on the ground, and vice versa. There are many ways in which the stitchery can be done, and here follow 3 ideas:

1 Several stitches such as feather, back and chain may be worked in varying lengths on each line, for an undulating effect.
2 Three different stitches may be worked, but embroider 1 only on 3 different lines, and repeat them in any order.
3 Use, say, feather stitch for the background and double knot stitch on the applied pieces.

Do not embroider the outline of the appliqué, but do add essential details, such as eyes to an animal, and windows and portcullis to a castle. (See diagrams.)

This method is very successful for people who are afraid to use colour. The palette is limited and the scheme is heraldically simple and direct. It is also a very durable method and it moves right away from tradition.

Really inexperienced students have carried out this kind of work successfully, and those who are not in favour of hand work simply embroider the lines with an electric sewing machine.

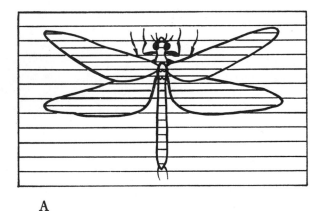

A

Appliqué with straight lines staggered

B

Appliqué with waved lines

Inlay Inlay requires patience and skill, and the beginner should work with a fabric which does not fray, such as felt. Make a design composed of shapes with simple outlines, and trace the main ones upon the background. With very sharp scissors cut out the shapes the merest fraction smaller than the tracing, and then tack the background firmly to a piece of paper. Tack round the holes, keeping about $\frac{1}{4}$ in. from the edge. Trace the pattern pieces upon felt of another colour, cut them a little larger than the tracing, drop them into the correct spaces in the background and tack them to the paper. With a fine matching cotton attach the pieces to the background with tiny fishbone stitches, taking care not to pierce the paper. (See diagram.) It is a good idea to use the dressmakers' thread which matches all colours. When all the parts have

been stitched, remove the tackings and prepare to add some embroidery. It seems pointless to embroider the edges of the shapes, so use slipped outlines, powderings and partial fillings. The photographs of two samplers of inlay show very different methods which were used by students who were preparing work for an examination. *The Pear* Audrey Mason (Plate VIII) was enriched with stitchery in the colours of the felt, which were red, white and blue. Careful adjustments of the quantity and density of the colours resulted in an effect which was far from being crude.
Bull's Eye Doris Warr (Plate VIII) is very different. Several rings of coloured felt were inlaid, and then a simple OP pattern of squares embroidered with dark crimson thread was worked over them. Note how the thickness of the stitchery decreases towards the centre.

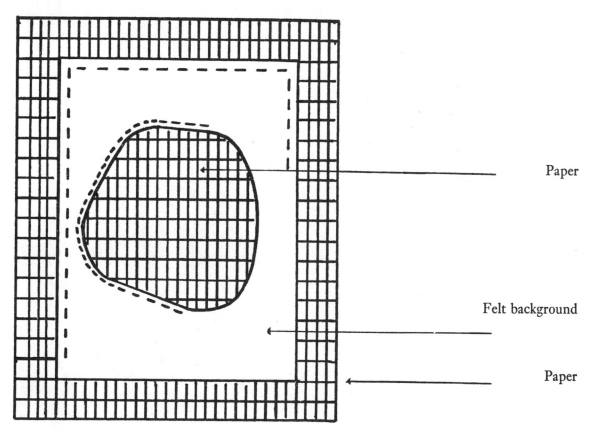

Paper

Felt background

Paper

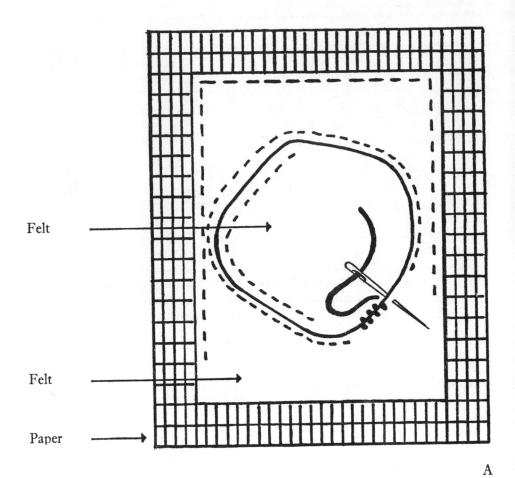

Felt

Felt

Paper

A

Prepared shape of felt with wedges of another
colour inlaid

B

Reverse Appliqué as it is sometimes called, could equally well be reverse inlay, and as the method falls between inlay and appliqué it was difficult to know where it should be placed in this book. It is used by the American Indians of Panama, who invent their designs as they work. Felt or some other non-fraying fabric is best for the beginner, but good firmly woven soft silks and also cotton fabrics can be used without difficulty. Draw a design composed of very simple shapes and trace it upon the fabric. Choose several more pieces of the same fabric in different colours, and tack them together (under the traced piece) very firmly. With sharp scissors, preferably ball pointed ones, carefully cut out a few pieces from the top layer only. Remember that some fabrics need turning under, and if a turning is required cut the shape smaller, to allow for this. Snip curves and corners and turn under with the needle, a little at a time. Hem the edges with small stitches which should be taken right through all the layers of fabric. Now cut pieces from 2 layers of fabric, and cut the under one further back than the top one, to avoid a 'step'. (See diagrams.) Stitch again right through all the layers. Carry on in this way until the design is complete and a few portions of each piece of fabric are exposed. Add surface stitchery if it is necessary. This method could be developed for tea-cosies (think how much laborious padding would be eliminated), for cushions, tops of boxes and even for costume and its accessories.

An adaptation of this method makes interesting and delicate room dividers, lamp shades, curtains, evening stoles and even book markers.

Take 2 pieces of fine fabric such as Indian silk, georgette or even nylon, of different colour and exactly the same size. Make a simple design, and mark the shapes 1 or 2, taking care to balance them nicely. Trace the areas marked 1 on the right side of the first piece of fabric. Reverse the design and trace the pieces marked 2 on the right side of the second piece. Tack the 2 pieces back to back, and add extra tacks between the design areas to prevent the under piece from slipping. Work side 1 first, with a matching

Four layers of felt sewn together

thread and very small stitches. Turn the embroidery over and work side 2 with matching thread. The work is quite effective at this stage, but the addition of crisp hand work is a further enrichment. Choose stitches which are pleasant on both sides, and if necessary whip or lace the wrong sides of the stitches. There must be no front or back, as both sides should be equally pleasing. This calls for neat beginnings and endings.

If the work is to be executed on a sewing machine trace the whole of the design upon the top fabric, then tack both pieces back to back and machine freely round each shape. Remember to cut away shapes from both the back and the front of the work, using ball-pointed scissors.

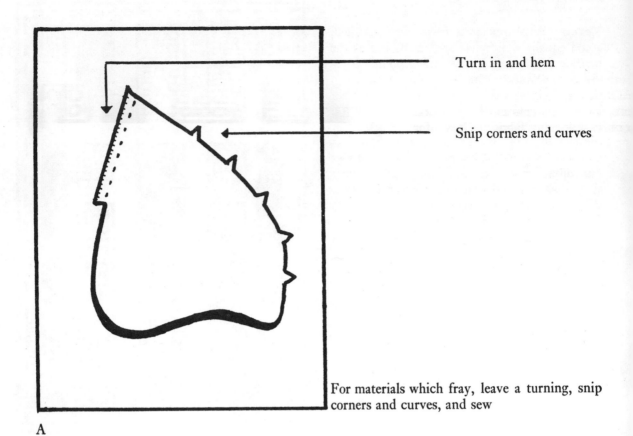

Turn in and hem

Snip corners and curves

For materials which fray, leave a turning, snip corners and curves, and sew

A

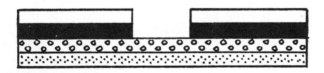

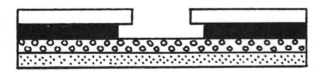

B

Cut under layer further back to avoid a deep step and long stitches

Side view through two cut layers of felt

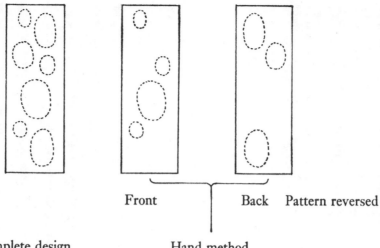

Front   Back   Pattern reversed

Machine method   complete design   Hand method

Striped Fabrics have been used effectively for many years, and although it seems as if no new ideas could possibly emerge, students are still finding interesting things to do. The simplest themes are often the most pleasing. One person traced a plain leaf shape upon a piece of narrow striped navy and white material. Inside the leaf shape she blotted out the white lines with navy stitchery, and added a partial outline, also in navy. The result was mock appliqué.

Tucking on narrow striped fabric is very pleasant. Use a light and a dark stripe for each tuck, and leave a pair of stripes between the tucks. Embroider the stripes between the tucks with a third colour before the tucks are made, and if a really stiff, ridged effect is required iron on a piece of adhesive backing when the embroidery is complete. Sometimes bugles or sequins are sewn between the ridges. The tucks must not be pressed, as they should stand upright. This method can be used for many embroidered articles, including boxes, belts, hangings, lampshades and even ecclesiastical furnishings.

80   Embroidery on striped fabric arranged to give the illusion of appliqué

73

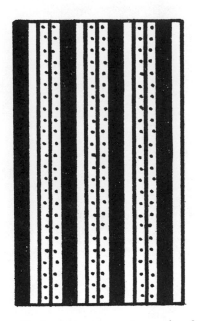

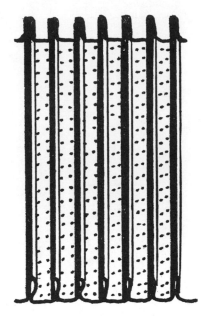

A

Embroider every other pair of stripes with
a third colour

B

Sew alternate navy and white stripes together

C

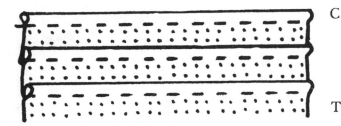

Tucks worked with running stitch

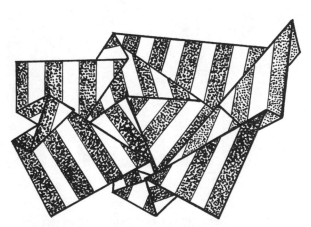

It is fun to fold striped fabric in all directions.
After folding it pin and press, then fix the folds
with running stitches worked in the colour of
one of the stripes. A student tried this idea with
a black and white boldly striped fabric, and although it was not taken out of the experimental
stage, I feel that it has possibilities.

Folded stripe experiment

74

Cut and Drawn Work of all kinds are lovely, and call for careful planning and skill in execution if the best results are to be obtained, yet they are often frowned upon by those who are searching for more up to date methods. If, however, we forget about the little mats and lacy tablecloths with which these embroideries are associated, and think of more unusual uses for them, it will be seen that it is possible to find a modern outlet for every kind of needlecraft.

Both hardanger and drawn thread work look attractive on lampshades, especially when the shade is lined with gaily coloured fine silk or cotton. Many modern designs are composed of squares of various sizes arranged freely over a shape, and hardanger embroidery just asks to be worked in squares.

Lined curtains and bedspreads are effective too, and many an enterprising young woman has enriched a simple dress with lined drawn thread work. The lining serves two purposes. It gives strength to the weakened portion of the fabric where the threads have been withdrawn, and it is very decorative, as a pretty lining enhances the beauty of the embroidery.

It is not necessary to adhere too closely to the traditional fabrics and methods. It is possible to withdraw threads from most evenly woven fabrics, and since the Kloster blocks of hardanger work are only satin stitches arranged in groups, there is really a wide choice of suitable materials. It is interesting to change the patterns in a border as one goes along, instead of working one pattern per border. Plan carefully, as it is easy to obtain a very muddled effect. Where borders run right round a cloth, mitre the patterns at the corners and use a different pattern on opposite sides. Squares are just as simple to fill with two, or even three patterns instead of one. Plan ideas on squared paper before embarking on a piece of work, as it is easier to correct faults in the drawing than in the embroidery.

Most cut and drawn work looks very effective in self colour, especially when it is lined. However, I do feel that it is right to experiment with all kinds of colour schemes, since so much depends on the individual taste and the effect which is required.

Double Running or **Holbein Work** and black work are especially favoured by those who like to count threads, but it does become a little tiring if nothing is done to add interesting textures or extra density of colour. Embroider some parts of the design with a much heavier thread than the one which is used for the greatest part of the work. For instance, it is an easy matter to use varying numbers of strands of cotton, say 1 for the main areas and 3 in carefully selected places. If laundering has not to be considered try fine silk threads and coarser woollen ones in the same piece of embroidery.

Raised Fillings Twisted lattice, honeycomb and many lace fillings take on a new look if various weights of thread are used for each filling. For honeycomb begin with a fine thread and work the bottom layer. Take a medium weight thread for the second layer and a coarse thread for the top one. Try it again but reverse the order of the threads. The same idea works for twisted lattice.

If there is no objection to adding extra weight to the middle of a lace filling it is possible to complete the filling and then work over the centre again and again until the desired height is obtained. For twisted lattice and honeycomb simply work the last layer over and over again in the place where a raised effect is required.

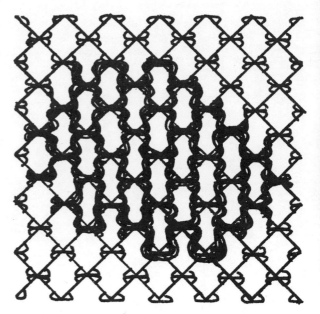

Raised Twisted Lattice

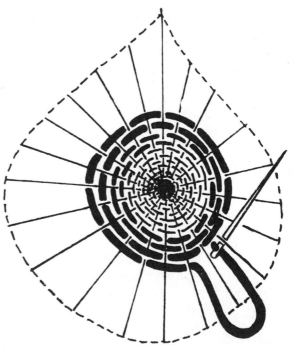

Needleweaving   A

76

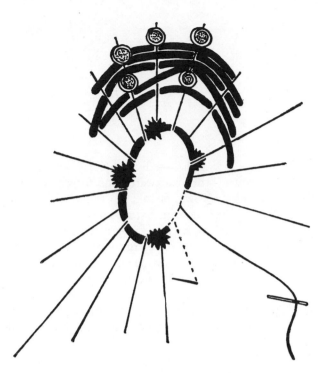

B Note the beads on the spokes

C Extra spokes on the edge of the shape

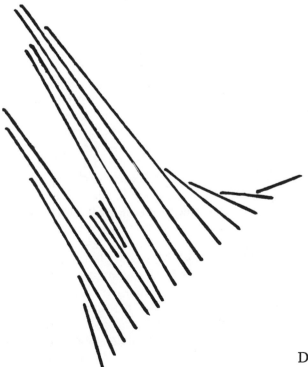

D Plan of spokes on difficult shape

77

Needleweaving From a simple and rather monotonous beginning, needleweaving has been developed during the last few years into a beautiful method which is so flexible that it almost outshines the rest. No longer is it considered necessary to withdraw threads from linen and other evenly woven fabrics in order to enrich the remainder with tiring repeated patterns in formal borders and stiff little motifs. Any kind of background is suitable. Long threads are placed where the needleweaving is required, and almost any kind of yarn is used for the woven part.

A For a hollow effect radiate the long threads from a given centre, and begin to weave at the centre with a fine thread. Gradually increase the weight of the thread until the outer edge is reached.

Since there is no law which says that needleweaving should be smooth, try the effect of weaving with all kinds of knitting yarns, hairy, knobbed, looped and those which vary in thickness every few inches.

B Thread beads, even large wooden ones, on the foundation lines, and weave round them until the shape is complete.

Radiate lines round a previously embroidered area, and do remember that the lines need not be of equal length. If any single lines remain, simply whip over and over them until they are covered, or leave them if a more spidery effect is required.

When shapes with an irregular outline are to be woven, it follows that shortest threads will be filled first, leaving gaps which cannot be worked in the usual way. Bring the needle up near to the first empty thread and weave to the end of the row. Then, depending on the function of the embroidery and the effect required, either turn neatly and work backwards and forwards at the ends of the rows, or take up the smallest possible amount of fabric before a new row is begun.

C Sometimes, as one progresses towards the outer edge of a shape, the space between the spokes becomes too wide and the weaving does not lie firmly. Add more spokes from the outer edge to the last row of weaving, taking care to push the needle well under the finished work, so that the weaving can flow in an uninterrupted way.

Needleweaving looks interesting if the space it is to occupy is padded. I like to sew on a pad of soft wadding and cover it with a piece of the background fabric.

Not all needleweaving needs to be completely solid. Open spaces and long whipped lines give a lace-like appearance to the work, which is often enhanced if pieces of coloured fabric are applied to the ground before the work is commenced.

D From the lacy effects it is a simple step to overlaid effects, and here needleweaving really becomes an art. Work bottom layers of weaving with a fine thread, and use gradually heavier threads as layer is superimposed upon layer. The idea was first suggested when students studied a cross section of a rather old gourd. The thread-like strands which held the seeds, and separated groups of them, seemed to ask to be interpreted in weaving.

E The sponge-like inner wall of the skin suggested a simple border, and now it has been discovered that no shape is really too difficult for this method provided that the work is planned carefully. If anything should go wrong, it is so easy to cut away the offending portion and begin again.

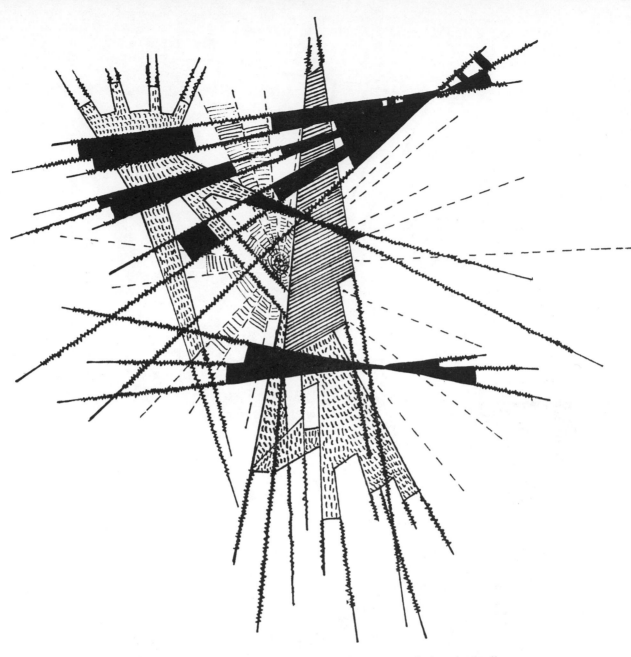

Layered needleweaving D

Note that most of the single lines are whipped

Key

≡≡≡	Lowest layer worked with finest thread
▨▨▨	1st overlay. Slightly heavier thread
≣≣≣	2nd overlay. Medium thread
▬▬▬	3rd overlay. Coarse thread

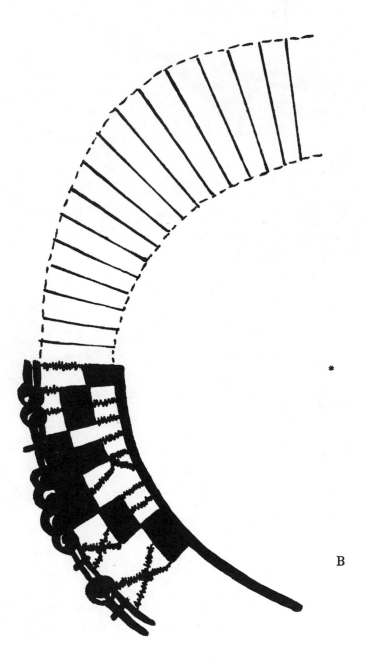

A

*

B

Needlewoven border adapted from the structure
of the skin of a gourd drawn in cross section.
Lines radiate from the centre *

The knobbed outer edge is knotted couching

Quilting So often the two main kinds of quilting are kept rigidly apart, yet it is possible to combine English and Italian methods, and even to add trapunto to complete a scheme. The design must be considered very carefully, as it is so easy to get a muddled effect, and then the method is condemned by the disappointed worker. The Italian quilted portion of the design is worked first and padded with quilt wool. Any trapunto quilting should be added next. Tack a layer of wadding and muslin behind the work and complete the design with English quilting.

The design shown in the first diagram is a difficult one for a beginner, but the cabbage in the second one is quite easy to work.

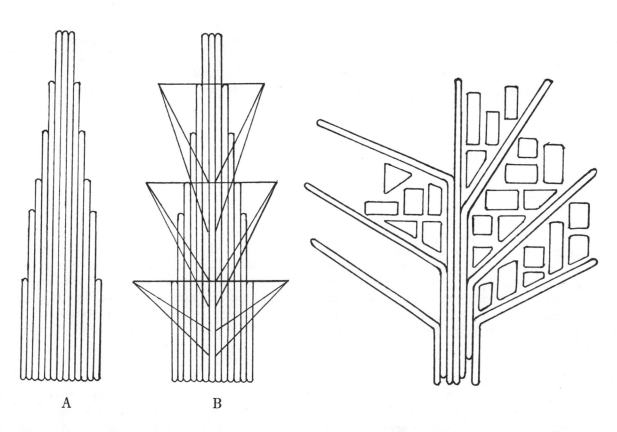

A   B

Idea for quilting based on the structure of the dome of a baseball field

Idea for quilting based on the structure of the back of a cabbage leaf

81

Mobiles Those who like fine embroidery, and who love to manipulate delicate fabrics, and to whom endless experiments are a source of enjoyment, find no problem too great to be solved when they embark upon mobiles. Since mobiles must be light enough to sway in the gentlest breeze, the fabrics must be chosen carefully, and the embroidered decoration, the stuffing and the materials used in the construction should be as delicate as possible. Beads are often heavy and should not be used too lavishly, but sequins are light and they give an air of luxury to the simplest units. Small units can be combined to form a complete scheme, and a team of workers of varied skill and experience finds this sort of communal work very rewarding. Since each person is responsible for one unit, it follows that each unit can be complete in itself and used as an individual creation should the need arise.

Mobiles composed of shoals of fishes, flights of birds and even of abstract shapes are rather uninteresting because they have been done so often. It is better to choose a theme, and envisage the mobile as a whole before breaking it down into separate portions. The size, the general arrangement of the units, a well balanced colour scheme and finally the design for each piece must be decided upon before any embroidery is begun. A three dimensional pattern made from pieces of paper stuck together with transparent adhesive tape should be constructed, as it will give a reasonable idea of the appearance of the finished article, and show where modifications and even additions are required. A group of embroiderers chose 'The Universe' as their theme, and decided that there should be a central portion to represent the solar system, with units representing the weather, land, sea and air arranged round it. The major problem was to find a way in which all these diverse units could be hung together in a meaningful and professional manner. One person found a very good solution to the problem. She decided that a simple hanging lampshade frame could be made into the sun, with floating rays of net and pieces of transparent fabric stretched across the base.

From this sun all the units could be suspended on nylon threads which would be passed through the sun and fixed to the sides of the frame. From a central position the weather could be suspended above the spheres which were to represent the moon and the earth. At strategic points, and a little lower down, the units representing land, sea and air would complete the mobile. The balance could only be corrected when the embroideries were complete, and the whole suspended on a ceiling light.

It was decided that gay tropical fishes darting through a transparent wave, and a pair of sea horses clinging to a piece of weed, would be the representatives of the sea. A tree full of exotic birds and a flower supporting butterflies were chosen to represent the air, and one unit of plant forms and one of fruits would represent the land.

Sketches for the designs were translated into paper patterns, and this was facilitated by the study of the patterns for children's toys. The choice of fabrics, stuffings and the method of making up were matters for the individual. Thin sheets of foam rubber were used to strengthen fine fabrics which were too flimsy to hold a good shape, fuse wire was sewn into seams, and best of all, frayed-out Lurex cloth was used as a stuffing for transparent fishes. Nets and frayed nylon were used for the tails and fins of fishes, and for the tails of birds, while stained pipe cleaners were used for a tree and for the bodies of butterflies.

Fairly thick foam rubber was covered with fine material and quilted with French knots for the centre of a large flower, and buttonhole rings joined together were found to be ideal for elder flowers. Nets and unspun nylon were used for the rainbow and fleecy clouds, and glittering beads secured on nylon thread made delightful raindrops.

This mobile proved that it is possible for imaginative embroiderers to create lovely work which owes very little to learning by rote. Each unit was highly individual, and problems for which there is very little guidance to be found, were overcome successfully.

The photograph of the butterfly and flower (Plate II) is worth studying, as it shows clearly what can be done by a skilful and patient worker.

The wings of each butterfly were embroidered right through two framed pieces of transparent fabric, between which small shapes of Lurex cloth were trapped. Stitches which could be made decorative on both sides were worked with great care, and the ends of the threads were hidden between the layers of material. Beads and sequins were used sparingly, but there were enough to make the wings iridescent. Fuse wire was buttonholed round the edge of each wing before the work was cut out of the frame, and the same kind of wire was used for legs and antennae. All the pieces of each butterfly were stitched to bodies made of brown pipe cleaners.

The centre of the flower has already been described. The petals were worked separately, and wired at the edges so that they would hold any shape into which they were pressed, and then they were attached to the centre piece. The stalk was added next, and finally silk sepals edged with bugles.

Angler fish

Cut 2 pieces of transparent fabric
Stuff lightly with frayed out Lurex fabric
Add fins before stuffing

Twisted wire

Frayed fabric edge

Opening for stuffing

Simple bird shape

Cut 2 pieces of fabric
Stuff lightly
Legs of coiled wire
Make tail of gathered net and add to the body

Opening for stuffing

Butterfly

2 layers of transparent fabric sewn together and embroidered right through. Beads form the irregular edges

83

4 Embroidered Boxes

Well made boxes are generally regarded as fascinating examples of the embroiderer's art, and they attract a good deal of attention when they are exhibited. Yet many people are hesitant to make one, and those who do usually confine their efforts to square or oblong boxes with plain hinged lids which are not fastened in any way. Probably they are afraid of the problems which a more difficult shape will present when the pieces have to be assembled. Actually it is no harder to make one shape than another. It is a matter of careful planning, and if the pieces are assembled in the correct order, no real problems will arise. Patience is needed, and willingness to unpick any part of the box which does not fit perfectly. Remember that any slipshod work will show.

A box must be firm, the lid must fit well, and the lining and fastening considered as carefully as the rest, so that they are part of a well balanced whole and not mere afterthoughts. Seams must be tight, straight and neat. The appearance of the seams separates amateur from professional work in no uncertain manner. I like a seam to look so tailored that there is no need to disguise it with cords or decorative stitchery. This is where the choice of material comes in. The threads of loosely woven fabric tend to gape when it is stretched over card, and stiff ones split when the seams are tightened. I prefer fabrics which give a little, and I have found that soft padding assists one to assemble the parts neatly.

Let us consider a simple square box stage by stage, beginning with:

Purpose We must decide upon the purpose of the box first, because purpose dictates to some extent shape, size, method and materials. Work boxes need to be reasonably large, in order to accomodate all the paraphernalia a needlewoman requires. Stud boxes should be small, and glove boxes must be large enough to hold gloves of all sizes comfortably.

Shape particularly of the interior, is dictated by purpose, but do remember that even if a very simple, oblong interior is required, it is possible to add interesting extras to the outside. Lids can be domed with extra padding, or made in sections, and fasteners can be beautiful as well as useful.

Size I suppose that, except for competitions, there is no upper or lower limit on the size of a box, unless storage or display space have some bearing on the matter. Purpose does influence the size, since a ring box needs to be just large enough to house its precious jewel, and a handkerchief box should be roomy as well as ornamental.

Pattern Having decided on the purpose, shape and size, make a three dimensional pattern with thick paper. Cut out all the pieces which will be required and fasten them together with strips of sellotape. Generally a few alterations have to be made, as the pattern is often far too big and out of proportion. Remember that this pattern is only a rough guide to the size of the shapes which will be required for the outer shell. The cardboard and the padding and the thickness of the material make such a difference to the measurements that the lid has often to be made larger than the base.

Method Having made a suitable pattern, the method must be decided upon, because the method will have some bearing on the choice of fabric. Embroidery which must be worked on counted threads requires a linen type fabric with evenly woven threads, while richer methods with metal threads and semi-precious stones should be worked on velvet or an expensive silk ground. Purpose will have some bearing on the method, as that which is suitable for a very feminine jewel box is not really right for a work box.

Design The design should be in keeping with the purpose of the box, and the fastening, if any, should be incorporated in it. Remember that the design should include sketches for the treatment of the interior of the box, as a quilted lining and pockets might be required. Trace the units which are to be embroidered on the exterior, and put the tracing aside until it is required.

Fabrics Some fabrics are so interesting on the wrong side that it is essential to decide which side is to be uppermost before pressing it, then *Tack* the outlines of all the outer shapes, including the lid and base, with a contrasting cotton, and leave at least $1\frac{1}{2}$ in. between each shape. Remember that the shapes might have to be enlarged later, and they will certainly require turnings. Match the grain on all the side pieces, especially if the material has a pronounced rib, and take care that none of the pieces are placed across the grain (see page 86).

Transfer the design, and frame the whole piece of material. Some materials will require a thin backing, especially if they have to support heavy embroidery.

Embroider the pieces, and where necessary press them on the wrong side before the work is removed from the frame.

Strawboard Choose a board of the correct thickness for the size of the box, and mark upon it the pieces for the base and sides only. Cut them out with a sharp knife and smooth the edges with emery paper.

Sides Cover the side pieces with wadding, and thin the wadding out at the edges. Mitre the corners of the wadding and stick the edges to the wrong side of the card. (See diagram.) Cut out the side pieces of fabric. Place the card with the wadded side downwards, with its edges lying on the tacking stitches, on the wrong side of the fabric. Mitre the corners of the fabric and stick the edges to the back of the card, first the top and bottom, and then the side edges. (See diagram.) If the work should slip out of position, or if it is not stretched tightly, simply take it off the card and begin again. When all the sides

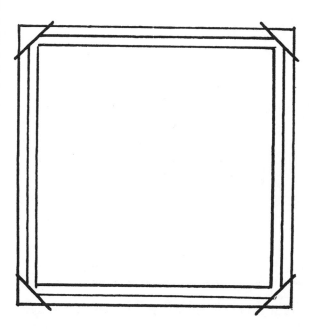

Back of card showing wadding at the edges

85

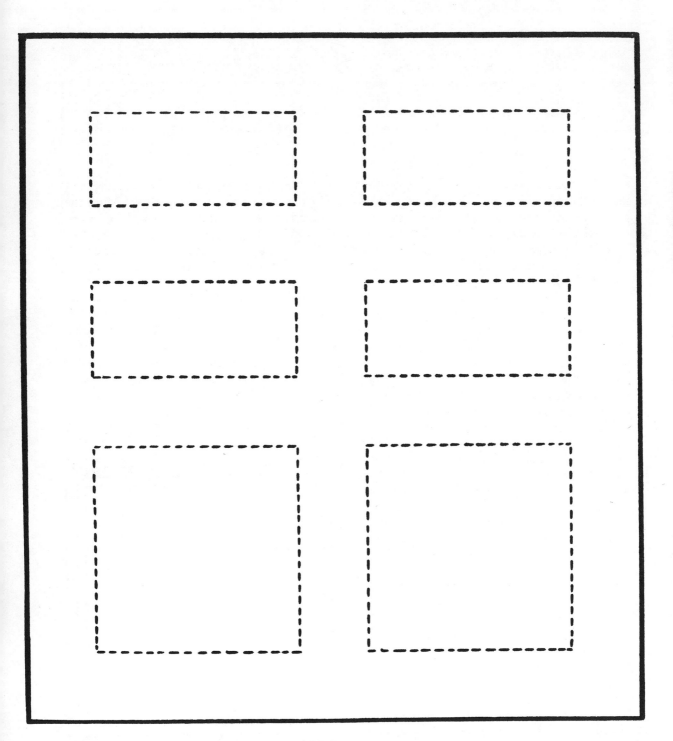

Pattern of the outer shapes tacked on the fabric

Lid and base 3 inch square. Sides $3'' \times 1\frac{3}{8}''$

have been stretched properly, remove the tackings, and leave the pieces to dry. Sew them together with ladder stitch, which is shown among the diagrams for patchwork. Pull the seams tight and sew up and down them several times if necessary. Do remember that ladder stitch is worked on the right side. You now have a hollow square.

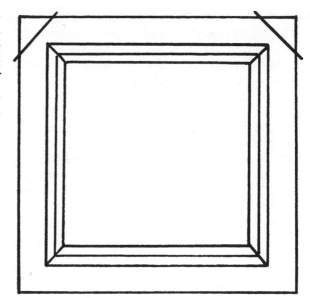

Wadded card placed on fabric

Three methods of attaching feet to base

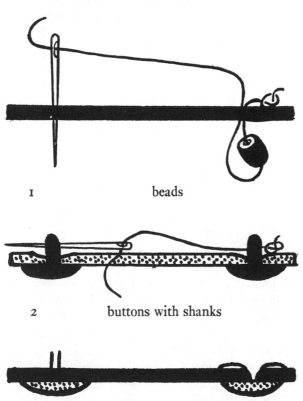

1   beads

2   buttons with shanks

3   button moulds

Base Make up like the sides, but use only the thinnest layer of padding. Mark the position of the feet on the outside of the base and attach them as suggested in the diagrams. Pierce the card with a stiletto, working from the outside. If beads are used take a linen thread and sew across the inside of the base from bead to bead. Secure the ends firmly and stick strips of adhesive tape across the long stitches for extra security.

If the shank of a button is so short that it is difficult to sew through it, gently scrape a well in the cardboard and thus reduce the thickness of it.

Metal button moulds are useful, as they need no sewing. Push the shanks through the card and bend them over. It is not necessary to use the underside of the button mould. Simply gather the covering fabric over the mould, and the base of the box will hold it in position.

Corners Tie the corners of the prepared base to the corners of the square, and then sew all round with ladder stitch. Remove the ties. If cording is required, add it now, so that the ends can be stuck down inside the box.

Hinges Mark their position on the inside of the back edge of the box. Take a piece of fabric $1\frac{1}{2}'' \times 4''$, fold it in half and machine the seam. Turn the tube right side out, and press it. It should measure $\frac{1}{2}'' \times 4''$. Stick the hinges in place, leaving 2 in. extending beyond the edge of the box. For extra firmness stick a strip of sellotape across them.

Fastener If a fastener is required, it should be worked and sewn to the front edge. Take the stitches right through the card and secure the ends with glue.

Piping It gives a professional finish to put piping round the top of the box. Use very fine string for the piping cord, and cover it with bias strips of the lining material. Make it by hand with running stitch, the exact length required, and turn in the fabric at each end so that there will be a neat join. Stick it in position, with the cord just touching the top of the box. Begin and end in a corner, and it will not be necessary to sew the join, because it will be almost invisible.

Lining Choose the fabric carefully, with due regard to colour and texture. It might echo one of the colours used in the embroidery, and it might be the same colour as the outer fabric. It might be completely different, so that when the box is opened one is startled.

Tack all the shapes required for the inside of the box, exactly as was done for the outer pieces. If quilting or any other decoration is required it should be done now, and pockets must be added before the lining is stretched over card.

Card Use a lighter weight board, and make the base first. It will need to be a fraction of an inch smaller than the outer one, and it should be padded quite thickly. Cut the first layer of wadding much smaller than the card, thin the edges and stick it in the centre of the shape. Cut another piece larger than the last one but a little smaller than the card, thin out the edges and

stick it over the first layer of wadding. Repeat in this way until the required thickness is obtained, and remember that the last layer must be large enough to fold over the edge of the card, and that it should be stuck on the back of the card only. Make sure that this inner base piece fits snugly inside the box, and allow for the thickness of the lining material. If the fit is not good, take off the last layer of wadding, and with emery paper gently smooth the edges of the card until it fits properly. Stick the lining on the padded card in the same way as the outer fabric, and after putting a generous amount of paste on the back, slip it into position and put a clean, heavy weight on it. Make up the side pieces, carefully adjusting the size of the boards until a very tight fit is obtained. It will be found that owing to the depth of the padding on the base, the inside boards will possibly need to be $\frac{1}{4}$ in. shorter in height than the outer ones. Do not sew the side seams. When the base is stuck firmly remove the weight, and paste the back of each of the side pieces. Slip them into position and press firmly. Hair clips (with tissue paper inside them to prevent damage to the fabric) should be placed over the edges of the box and left in position until the sides are firm.

Lid The board should rest firmly on the edges of the box, and it must be cut from the sheet which was used for the outer pieces. Measure the box carefully, as the thickness of both the card and the wadding will have made it slightly larger than the original pattern. Pad the lid well, and stick on the fabric. Make a narrow piping and stick it round the edges. If a fastener has been sewn on the side of the box, make a loop of fabric or cord and stick it in position, as shown in the diagram. Stitch it firmly to the raw edges of the binding and sellotape the ends. Mark the position of the hinges and stick them to the lid, allowing only enough play between the box and the lid to ensure a firm fit. Sew the sides of the hinges to the edges of the piping and fix them securely with adhesive tape. (See diagram.) Make up the lining over finer card, stick it in position and clip it until it is quite firm. It is often necessary to sew round the lid, to make it really firm. Use a strong but fine thread and work from side to side under the piping.

Velcro and press studs sewn on a piece of embroidered fabric make good substitutes for a button and loop fastener.

There are many ways in which the pattern of a box can be adapted from the basic one, and the first step is to make different kinds of lids.

Lids which fit over the lower part of the box need side pieces, and the simplest ones are just a slightly larger box in reverse.

1 Finish the lower part of the box. No hinges or fasteners are required.
2 Make the lining of the lid, which must be finished with a strong, smooth fabric. Sew the pieces together with ladder stitch, making sure that the fabric is inside and that the complete shell fits tightly.
3 Make up the OUTSIDE of the lid. The pieces of card must be a little larger than those used for the lining. Sew all the pieces together with ladder stitch, with the fabric on the outside. Slide the complete shell over the lining and sew the bottom edges together.

Lids which rest INSIDE the box should be made slightly smaller than the base. The lining of the box is cut about $\frac{1}{4}$ in. shorter than the outer shell, to make a ledge upon which the lid will rest.

Lid of simple box

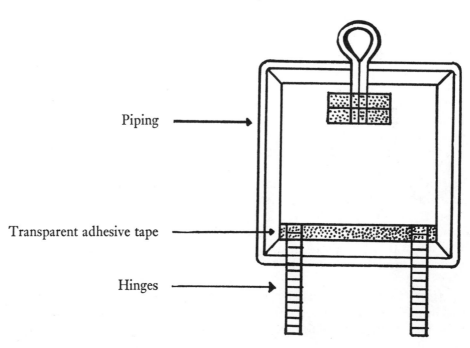

Piping

Transparent adhesive tape

Hinges

Small Circular Boxes Cut off a piece of card from a tube of the required diameter, and pad it lightly. Make a pattern with paper which is 1 in. deeper than the ring of cardboard and $\frac{1}{2}$ in. longer than the circumference. Use the pattern as a template for marking the fabric. Embroider the material, machine the short seam on the wrong side and press the seam flat. Draw the fabric over the cardboard shape, adjust the fitting, and stick the edges inside the ring at the top and the bottom. Cut a circle of cardboard for the base, cover it as for other boxes and add feet if they are required. Sew it to the ring with ladder stitch. Place 1 or 2 hinges if they are necessary. Stick in the lining for the base in the manner which has already been described. For the side lining take a smaller, thinner circle of card, or make one from postcards, cover it, and insert. Make up the lid and attach it to the box. If a fastener is required it is quite satisfactory to sew the base of a tiny press stud to the rim of the box, and its upper half to the lining of the lid.

A box with the top and sides in one piece was designed and made by one of my students, Constant Norris. It was one of a pair which were to be a gift for the golden wedding of some friends, and it was worked on a rich brown Thailand silk with all kinds of gold thread. (See plates III and IV.)

To Make Tack out the pattern on the fabric as shown in the diagram, trace the design and embroider it. Since the sides are in one piece with the top, it is possible to have a design which flows from the top and down the sides, as there are no awkward seams to spoil the arrangement. Take a piece of cardboard on which the shape has been drawn accurately and with a sharp knife score it deeply on the dotted lines. (See diagram.) Fold the sides upwards and fix them in position with small pieces of transparent adhesive tape, then take strips of tape right round the box to strengthen it and ensure a good shape. Cut the wadding in one piece slightly larger than the pattern, lightly paste it to the base and draw the sides upwards, giving them a dab of paste to secure them. Thin out the top edges, fold them over the card and stick them inside the box. Now cut out the embroidered fabric, leaving $\frac{1}{4}$ in. turnings. Back stitch the side seams by hand and mitre the corners. Turn the fabric right side out, press the seams open very carefully, and draw it over the padded box. Make any adjustments which are needed to ensure a really tight fit, then turn the edges over the top of the card and stick them down. This piece is the lid. Make the lining as for other boxes, and pipe the edge.

The lower half of the box is made exactly like the lid, but it must be a little smaller. Make the cardboard shape just loose enough to slide into the lid easily, as the wadding and the covering will increase its size. Sew the feet to the base before the lining is inserted.

This method is not easy, but it is worth trying.

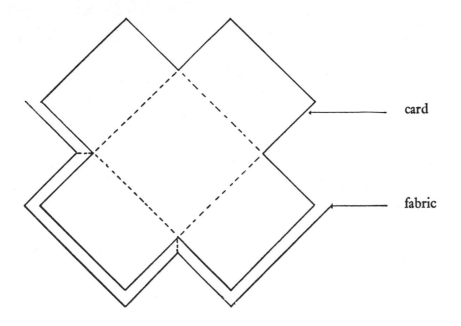

card

fabric

Plan of box with sides and top in one piece.

Score card on dotted lines

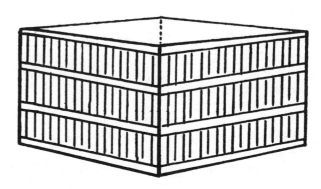

Cardboard shape held in position by transparent
adhesive tape

The box by Honor Costelloe shown on Plate VI was very beautifully embroidered on muted cream and coffee coloured silk with beads of various sizes and shapes. The box is hexagonal, and the colour scheme is counterchanged. Inside the base there is a detachable stiffened centre piece which divides it into 6 compartments. The lid is small enough to slip inside the box and rest on this divider.

The main interest is in the lid, which is actually another box. It has shallow sides, and from the sides separate petal shapes spring upwards and are held in position with a beaded ring. When the ring is removed, the petals fall back to reveal a shallow compartment.

Another interesting box, Doris Warr (Plate II), excited admiration for its very neat finishing and the beauty of the lining. It is a simple square box, with a hinged lid which is not fastened but held in position with a weighted loop. The outer fabric is silver grey linen embroidered with several kinds of thread with irregular couched fillings and line stitches. The lining is pale turquoise silk, quilted with embroidered covered buttons, like the handsome buttoning on good furniture. Suspended on the back edge is a small scented sachet with a piped edge, made of the same turquoise silk.

Sometimes in spite of every effort to prevent seams from gaping, the stitches show and something has to be done to neaten the box. Cords are useful, but it strengthens the seams if embroidery is used instead.

Double knot stitch grips both sides of the seam, and its thick centre covers most irregularities. If the stitch alone does not cover the faults completely, thread it like threaded back stitch to increase its width.

A

B

101 Crossed Double Knot is firmer than the usual form, as the first movement is repeated twice. Work the stitches close together if a thick edge is necessary.

A

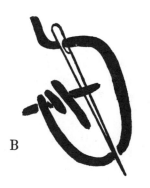

B

102 Whipped Double Knot closes gaps well because it has a thick centre. After making the first part of the stitch, whip it twice before proceeding to the last movement.

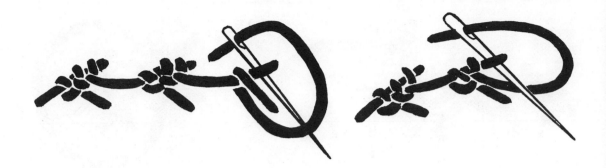

103 *Heavy Knot* Repeat the last movement as often as necessary and place the stitches close together.

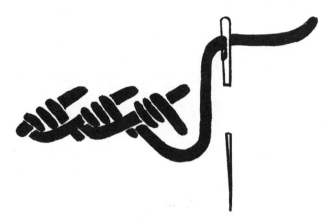

104 *Rope Knot* Repeat the whipping as often as required to make firm edge. Work the stitches close together.

It follows that all these variations of double knot can be added to, and if necessary laced as for threaded back stitch. Do not leave long loops when lacing, and conversely do not pull the lacing so tight that it makes the stitch narrower.

Conclusion

Many of the traditional kinds of embroidery, though undeniably beautiful and durable, do not satisfy absolutely the embroiderer who wishes to be creative. Inlay, patchwork and needleweaving, for instance, give a rather rigid appearance to the freest of designs, and at first glance it seems to be impossible to adapt or rejuvenate these somewhat mechanical methods. But it is possible, if sufficient thought is given to the problem on hand, to find a new approach to every kind of needlecraft. In this book I have tried to prove that there is a vast new field waiting to be explored by those who wish to venture along the almost untrodden paths of creative needlecraft, and that no one need ever wonder what to do next.

Many people still fear that someone, somewhere, will pronounce their efforts to be incorrect if they deviate slightly from a traditional form. It is difficult to convince them that new ventures in any field, from fashion to architecture, are usually condemned, and that since nothing remains unchanged from generation to generation it is no use worrying about the critics.

One has only to give a cursory glance at the history books, and at displays in museums, to discover how styles and methods have changed from age to age. But just as there are typical styles by which we recognize the work of different countries, and of different periods, there are also individuals in each nation who produce uncharacteristic work. How refreshing it is to find embroidery which was created by those wonderful people who refused to be bound by the confines of their country and their times. There must be many embroiderers in the world today who, if given the slightest encouragement, will eagerly embark upon work which will prove to posterity that needlecraft was a living art in the twentieth century.

PLATE VIII

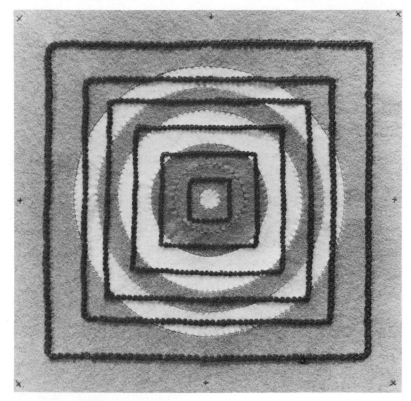

Inlay
Doris Warr

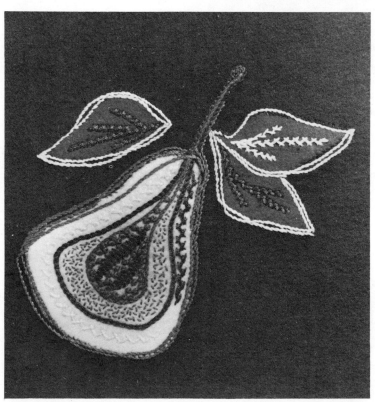

Inlay
Audrey Mason

THE END